Sources and Translation Series
of the Russian Institute
Columbia University

Alexander Pushkin

THREE COMIC POEMS

Gavriiliada
Count Nulin
The Little House in Kolomna

Translated and edited by William E. Harkins

Ardis / Ann Arbor

The Russian Institute of Columbia University sponsors the "Sources and Translation Series of the Russian Institute" in the belief that important works of Russian history, literature, and criticism as well as memoirs and other source materials not previously available in English in complete form should be made available to specialists and to a general reading audience. It is hoped that these publications will contribute to the knowledge and understanding of Russian history and culture, as well as to enhanced respect for the craft of translation.

CONTENTS

PREFACE

It is often said that Pushkin is untranslatable by virtue of the extreme precision of his Russian style, but it is perhaps not immodest to add that his poetry of wit may be a bit more translatable than other parts of his poetic heritage. English has a rich tradition of poetry of wit, and it was Lord Byron whose *Don Juan* served Pushkin as a model for much of his humorous verse.

With Pushkin, as with Byron, the verse form and rhyme are closely bound up with the humor and wit, and the translator who might be inclined to produce a free, unrhymed translation for a meditative lyric has little choice but to adhere, more or less closely, to the metrical and rhyming patterns Pushkin has set down in his humorous poetry.

All translation requires compromises and sacrifices. Readers who do not read Russian but who may be interested in following the course of the original somewhat more closely than any translation (except a trot) can do, may find help in the notes provided here: these comment on seemingly unavoidable distortions or alternative choices adopted in making the present rendering. Resort to notes might seem to argue that the task is indeed a hopeless one, for few if any of these notes call attention to any possibly felicitous renderings. But, all things being equal, a fairly critical posture in the notes seemed most appropriate.

I trust that no apology is required for bringing these three poems together under one cover. Insufficient critical attention has been devoted to Pushkin's quite considerable comic talents, although he may well have been the greatest

7

of Russian humorous poets. If the spirit of the blasphemous *Gavriiliada* does not quite accord with that of the other two poems, then I might add that it is the least available of the three works in older English renderings. The translation published by Max Eastman many years ago is so rare that I have never been fortunate enough to see a copy.

I owe a very great debt to my friend and colleague Professor Richard Gregg of Vassar College for his close criticisms of all three texts and his many helpful suggestions. In the case of "Count Nulin" so much of his advice has been incorporated in the final version as to make him the virtual co-author of that translation.

William E. Harkins
Columbia University

PUSHKIN AS COMIC POET

Devotees of Pushkin's poetry may well be surprised to hear him described as a humorous poet. Yet the three poems presented here, taken with the humorous and satiric digressions in his "novel in verse," *Eugene Onegin*, form a significant and quite substantial line of development in Pushkin's work. True, this line may not be so significant or profound, ultimately, as the line represented by "The Gypsies," "Poltava," and finally by what is probably Pushkin's greatest work, "The Bronze Horseman," a line of expression that attempts to unmask the romantic myth of the individual in his relation to society and state. But still it is a quite substantial one. Comic and satiric poems were essential stages in the development of Pushkin's creative imagination, and if the blasphemous *Gavriiliada* seems to result from little more than an adolescent preoccupation which had to be written out so that more serious things could then be undertaken, "Count Nulin" and "The Little House in Kolomna" represent an attempt to found a poetry, if one of rather frivolous humor, in everyday Russian reality (in contrast to the romantic escapism that still infects "The Gypsies" right up to the poem's end). These three poems, spread over the period 1821-1830, punctuate it in a fashion suggesting that they played the psychological role of a comic release for their creator; they jested, mocked and parodied so that the poet might go on to more serious things, and it is possibly of significance that both "Count Nulin" and "The Little House in Kolomna" were written during extremely productive periods of creative activity on Pushkin's part.

Pushkin's lyrics, it is true, take individual feelings seriously and more or less at their own evaluation. But whenever he depicts the world about him, in drama or narrative, then irony, humor or satire are almost inevitably present. Only

9

when he hits (and this is rare) the bedrock of some solid moral absolute, as he does in fully unfolding the character of Tatyana in *Onegin*, or when he gives some surreal fantasy form and life, as in "The Bronze Horseman," does humor seem to be put entirely aside. This is one important reason, no doubt, why he preferred the Shakespearean chronicle play as a model for the nascent Russian theater, rather than the French neoclassic drama, because the former gave licence to comic expression even in the midst of tragedy.

The chief device of Pushkin's humor is his dry irony, the pose of an urbane sophisticate, judging all that fails to come up to his own high if rather empty standard. This is of course a pose, and rarely if ever excludes on Pushkin's part an appreciation of true worth and feeling; such irony may interest us relatively little today, and it is important to see that, as Pushkin's creation matures, it becomes less and less significant. "Count Nulin" is perhaps the high point of its expression; in this poem everything is viewed through the refracting light of a cold and blase, if far from tired irony. In "The Little House of Kolomna," the treatment of the mother, the old servant Fyokla, and the poet's urbane disclaimer and disengagement at the end are all typically Pushkinian ironies, but other things in the poem are accepted with less detachment and reserve: the poet's youth in Kolomna, where he once had lived, the digression about Countess X and her unhappy life, and, most important, perhaps, the characterization of the heroine, Parasha. In Parasha Pushkin seems to admire a free spirit untrammeled by authority or convention who has the sense and the integrity to arrange her life as she pleases and is best able. No doubt she is a figure of comedy, like the rest, but she is not the target of sarcasm or ironic contempt. *Eugene Onegin* (1823-1830), written over approximately the same period as the one we are considering here, shows a similar development, and the maximum point of ironic attitude for Pushkin is doubtless the very beginning, when he was still fascinated by Byron and his *Don Juan*. The ending of the work, with its exaltation of Tatyana's world of solid ethical values, is quite sober and unironic.

10

Pushkin's ironic attitude toward the characters he creates and their world touches on another sphere in which we are more ready to give him our admiration today: this is his poetic self-consciousness, his continual awareness of the literary process and his irony over it. This constant undercutting of literary effect, often known as "romantic irony," and renamed "laying bare the device" by the Russian Formalist critics of the 1920's, leads at its culmination to a kind of metapoetry, poetry about the poetic process itself, of which the introduction to "The Little House in Kolomna" is a superb example. Pushkin's metapoetic digressions are invariably humorous, of course (in contrast to lyrics such as "The Poet"), and never betray the seriousness with which he took his poetic gift and its exercise, or the very serious literary polemical exchanges in which he was continually involved in the late 1820's and early 1830's. These polemics were directed in part against critics such as Polevoy and Nadezhdin who were seeking to import a foreign, overblown Romanticism into Russian letters. Pushkin fought the new trend in vain: although his own late, anti-romantic works are far better remembered today than such callow novels as Zagoskin's *Yuri Miloslavski* (1829), a shoddy attempt to Scottize Russian history, still in his own time the reading public much preferred Zagoskin to any of Pushkin's writings after the youthful romantic ones such as "The Prisoner of the Caucasus" (1822) and "The Fountain of Bakchissaray" (1823). For the development from Classicism to Romanticism in Russian letters never admitted the cult of the vulgar, the everyday, or the prosaic. All that was literary must perforce be noble and marked by pretention, and the unique combination that Pushkin achieved in "Count Nulin" and "The Little House in Kolomna" of the banal, the comic, the frivolous and the realistic, was simply not apprehended as poetic, either by the reading public or even the best critics of the time, caught up in the new vogue of Romanticism.

The three poems included here see the development of metapoetic irony: it is relatively restrained and infrequent in the *Gavriiliada* (where it is connected mostly with the undercutting digression, which helps to break up the uniform monotony of epic tone), but becomes more frequent in "Count Nulin," where there is an ironic reference to the problem of stylistic tone ("Pray pardon the prosaic phrase"), and where literature and the stage both come in for criticism in the course of the poem. In "The Little House in Kolomna" it is virtually the subject of the poem itself, and in this work the reader may conceivably take the story as little more than an illustration of the literary attitude set forth in the brilliant introduction, which opens the door to a new poetic universe: poetry can be fashioned by a poet out of anything, even out of the frivolous, the trivial and the banal. The art of poetry lies partly in form and style, as the introduction suggests, partly in craftsmanship, and not (*pace* such lyrics by Pushkin himself as "The Prophet" and "The Poet") in a divine gift: such poetry is only contemned here ("And gone to seed Parnassus"). No doubt this is partly a pose on Pushkin's side (his lyrics clearly belie such an attitude), but it is a pose that he finds quite acceptable for creative purposes.

Parody, even self-parody, is another important element of humor in these poems. The *Gavriiliada* is an example of the mock-epic, a parodic genre. "Count Nulin" was originally conceived as a parody on Shakespeare's "The Rape of Lucrece," though this intention appears to have been weakened in the execution. Parasha and her mother in "Kolomna" recall in parodic fashion Tatyana and Mme. Larina in *Eugene Onegin*: the scene in which Parasha gazes at the moon is the bathetic equivalent of Tatyana's moon-gazing in Chapter II of *Onegin*, while Parasha's fondness for sentimental novels recalls Tatyana's adolescent reading taste.

Pushkin's fondness for digression is well known, and all three of these poems contain numerous examples. No doubt digression ("romantic" irony) as such is essentially an ironic device, undercutting the tone which builds up as the culmination of the literary process. But it is important to realize that Pushkin's digressions in these poems (unlike many in *Onegin*) are usually *not* comic: they are lyric, sometimes poignantly so. The reminiscence in the *Gavriiliada* of the playing fields of the poet's youth spent at the Lyceum in Tsarskoe Selo, or the sound of carriage bells in "Count Nulin," or the poet's recollection of Parasha's house, no longer standing in "Kolomna," convey a keen sense of personal involvement and of individual fate. Hence, though the procedure of the digression itself suggests the comic, the practice is rather one of compensatory balance: the more comic the poet's subject, the less humorous the digressions. *Onegin* is scarcely comic in subject (in spite of the social comedy it involves), but it becomes a comic poem (in a limited sense) by virtue of certain of its digressions. On the other hand, the comic is constantly checked by the digressions in the three poems we are considering, lest it get out of hand. For the esthetics of poetry for Pushkin lie deeper than surface comedy; their focus for him is on creativity: the poet's ability to create a congruent world, a world identifiable with our own world in its sensitive intuitions and perceptions and its understanding of human character and human conflict, but a world that is removed through the special genius and technique which animate it, through its display of art and artifice.

The element of anecdote is strong in Pushkin's humorous poems. Both "Count Nulin" and "Kolomna" are narratives based on comic anecdotes. Elements of comic misapprehension or misunderstanding play a large role in the story development of these poems. In "Count Nulin" the count mistakes his hostess' flirtatiousness for a more serious interest. In "The Little House in Kolomna" the servant is a man in woman's clothing who passes for a woman in spite of his unwomanly ways in housekeeping. Only in the *Gavriiliada* do we have an epic rather than an anecdotal type of story structure: the rivals for Mary's affection do combat in order to win her. Comedy here proceeds more from character and situation: Joseph is too old to pay heed to his young bride; God is an old lecher who wishes to seduce her; Gabriel is accustomed to cuckold the very God he serves, etc. This progression from epic to anecdotal is significant for Pushkin's later work: we find anecdotal tales, whether comic or serious, in the *Tales of Belkin* or "The Queen of Spades," and even "The Bronze Horseman" is a kind of extended anecdote, though the last two named works embody epic elements as well. The anecdotal element is also marked in the two plots that, as tradition has it, Pushkin offered to Gogol, which subsequently served as bases for the latter's *Inspector-General* and *Dead Souls.*

It may be superfluous to speak of the comic characterization that Pushkin achieves in these three poems, richest in "Count Nulin." All the characters in that poem are quite real and vivid (perhaps most vivid are the minor ones: the servants Picard and Parasha). The self-satisfied, indulgent husband (even more indulgent to himself than to his wife), the foppish, empty-headed Nulin ("Count Nocount"), the silly but resolute wife—all are figures somewhere between characters of fixed humor and characters of true psychic depth. None develops, but all of them unfold, and their admirable quality is in the rightness of the details chosen to reveal their natures. Scarcely less good are the characters in "Kolomna," especially the mother and the old cook. The daughter Parasha is perhaps less clearly realized, but since her true story had to be told between the lines, this is no doubt inevitable. The same restriction applies, of course, to the new cook she hires.

Letting important details narrate themselves between the lines is a typical form of Pushkinian irony. It is most marked in his *Tales of Belkin* and "The Queen of Spades." But in "The Little House in Kolomna," or at the very end of "Count Nulin," we have wonderfully comic examples of this ironic mode.

The *Gavriiliada* is a classic example of the mock-epic or burlesque travesty, strongly influenced by the French models of the genre in the work of Voltaire and Parny. But this form had become outmoded by the 1820's, and Pushkin discarded it after he finished his blasphemous mock-epic poem. In "Count Nulin" and "Kolomna" we have examples of a quite new, mixed genre, still carrying certain vestiges of the mock-heroic (as in the depiction of Nulin's progress toward the heroine's bedroom, or the scene in "Kolomna" in which the widow runs home to find the new cook shaving), but mingling these with elements of the typical, the real, the banal and the picturesque. This mixture is comic in its very discrepancy, of course, but, had the ironic and mock-heroic elements been discarded entirely, it could have served as the ba-. sis for a poetry of everyday realism. *Onegin* goes somewhat farther in this direction, but Pushkin was hardly prepared to go the whole road, for realism of narrative tone would have involved for him loss of the architectonic effect of a constructed poetry, and this he hardly wanted to give up.

In concluding, it may be appropriate to comment on the relation of the verse form to the poetic wit. The constantly shifting, arbitrary rhyme scheme with little or no intrinsic connection with the matter under discussion (in "Count Nulin" this shifting rhyme scheme even crosses the section boundaries of the poem) helps to undercut, ironically, the matter discussed and support the playful, frivolous tone. The versatility of rhyme, with triple rhymes in all three poems, not only gives brilliance but firms up the external structure at the expense of the internal one and again supports the ironic pose. In "The Little House in Kolomna" the couplet rhymes at the end of each stanza, as in *Onegin*, give a striking filip that is often very funny.

GAVRIILIADA

Pushkin's parodic epic, the blasphemous and mildly pornographic *Gavriiliada* (or "Epic of Gabriel") is, like his equally notorious and rather more scabrous ballad, "Tsar Nikita," the fruit of youthful high spirits and a possibly excessive enthusiasm for French free thought. The work has a number of burlesque models in the French tradition, equally blasphemous, including Voltaire's *La Pucelle d'Orleans*, and Parny's *La Guerre des dieux*, *Le Paradis perdu*, and *Galanteries de la Bible*; Parny and Voltaire were two of Pushkin's favorite authors, and with all of these works the *Gavriiliada* has a number of striking parallels. Milton's *Paradise Lost* may have helped inspire Pushkin to compose Satan's moving account of how he taught Adam and Eve the art of love.

No copy of the *Gavriiliada* in Pushkin's handwriting has survived, and some authorities persistently denied his authorship of the poem. But the facts are fairly clear. Pushkin's notes contain several references to the subject itself and even a few lines of rough draft, while his letters of the period (spring, 1821) make a number of veiled hints about the progress of the work. Pushkin was required by his nominal position in the Civil Service (which he retained even during his exile) to attend Russian Orthodox church services, at which the congregation stood for several hours in unheated sanctuaries, and his letters as well as several poetic fragments of the period leave no doubt that he found this chore an onerous one. The *Gavriiliada* was a natural release for the resentment he felt, not only against his duties with regard to the Church, but against the whole system and the officials who kept him in exile in the south of Russia.

At the time, Pushkin was stationed in Kishinev in Bessarabia, the headquarters of General Insov, his superior. Pushkin had been assigned as a secretary under Insov in punishment for a number of too liberal poems and epigrams at the expense of the regime of Alexander I. In fact he was a political exile, sent to the south and prohibited from publishing so that he could be kept in line. Although Insov treated him like a son, lent him money from time to time (his pay usually came late and was always insufficient), permitted him occasional travel, and required him to do absolutely no work— none of this reconciled the poet to his position. He could neither retire from the hated Civil Service nor assume any of the perquisites of a writer that he felt to be his just desert. Though life in Kishinev was not without its consolations (its almost oriental color and the beauty of its wives and daughters, whom Pushkin assiduously courted), still the town was a dirty, boring hole, rife with fist fights and intrigue and totally without culture, including the theater and ballet Pushkin loved. It was a great relief to him when, in July, 1823, he was finally permitted to move on to Odessa, a town with good Russian society and an opera.

The *Gavriiliada* soon began to circulate in copies among Pushkin's friends and acquaintances, and it was generally recognized as Pushkin's work. Vyazemski wrote to an acquaintance that he had received his copy from Pushkin himself. In fact the poem spread so widely that it finally involved the author in difficulty. This happened in 1828, after Pushkin had been brought back from exile and "pardoned" by the new emperor, Nicholas I, but was still being kept under close police supervision. The house servants of a certain Captain Mitkov, a retired army officer, testified to the ecclesiastical authorities that their master was in possession of a copy of the scurrilous poem. A special commission of three was appointed in April, 1828, to investigate the matter, and the emperor himself was kept informed of the investigation's progress. Pushkin was interrogated by the commission, but twice denied his authorship; he did admit to having seen a copy of the poem, which he said he had copied as a student in the Lyceum at Tsarskoe Selo in 1815 or 1816 (an admission made, evidently, in case any copy in his handwriting was still circulating). No charge was made against him, and Pushkin hoped he was out of danger. To cover his tracks, however, he wrote to Vyazemski on September 1, 1828, mentioning the interro-

18

gation and adding that he might have to pay for "someone else's pranks, unless Prince D. Gorchakov should return from the other world to claim his property." Gorchakov, the known author of several scabrious poems, was dead and his reputation already damaged, and Pushkin evidently hoped to throw the authorities off the track; either the letter might be opened (as had already happened to him on more than one occasion), or Vyazemski might take the hint and repeat the story to others, since he was well aware of the poem's actual authorship. But the strategem did not avail. The emperor, who understood that he could maintain his superiority over the poet best by appearing to be magnanimous toward him, instructed the commission to summon Pushkin and remind him that the emperor knew Pushkin personally and trusted him. Nicholas then asked for the poet's cooperation in establishing who had written such a "piece of garbage" and thus done injury to Pushkin's own good name. This clever gambit placed Pushkin in an awkward position, and he finally asked the commission to permit him to write to the emperor directly concerning the matter. The request was granted, and Pushkin wrote to Nicholas; this letter and the emperor's reply have not been preserved. But on December 31 Nicholas indicated that the case was closed; it seems evident that Pushkin must have confessed his guilt and, as once before in 1826, appealed for the emperor's clemency.

Captain Mitkov had two of his house servants drafted into the army (one was first flogged) and, though the emperor had given personal orders that no reprisals be permitted against the servants who had denounced Mitkov, Nicholas failed to intervene: it was a serf-owner's legal right, after all, to select those of his serfs who were to do military service, an obligation which at that time lasted for twenty-five years.

Though we cannot show that Pushkin suffered from the affair, it must be said that the whole business played into the emperor's hand and enabled the monarch to continue to enact with entire success the curious and self-appointed role of Pushkin's patron, censor and jailer, combined in one.

*

19

Unlike "Count Nulin" and "The Little House in Kolomna," which are mixed in genre, the *Gavriiliada* is a classic example of the mock-epic or burlesque travesty. In general its genre can be defined as that of high burlesque: a vulgar subject treated in a lofty style and manner (as opposed to a lofty subject treated vulgarly), and thus it corresponds to the genre represented in English literature by such works as Pope's *Rape of the Lock*; the Russian prototype of this genre, insofar as one existed, was Vasili Maykov's *Yelisey, or Bacchus Infuriated* (1771), a long narrative poem in which a drunken coachman is the hero of a series of comic and ribald adventures, recounted in an amusing mock high style. As often happens in this genre, the style is not quite pure, and Maykov descends from time to time to colloquial and vulgar expression for the sake of comic effectiveness. This descent is not so marked in Pushkin's *Gavriiliada*: the poem is, for the most part, a smoothly flowing stream of high-style language with a number of Church Slavonicisms and only an occasional descent into the realm of the colloquial or the pithily expressive. Hence the poem, which in any event must be regarded as a youthful escapade on Pushkin's part, can hardly be said to be his most successful form, and it lacks the colorful, colloquial "realism" of the later comic poems, "Count Nulin" and "The Little House in Kolomna." Still it would be very wrong to dismiss the *Gavriiliada* as merely an immature work. Granted, it is uneven, and parts of it suffer from excessive smoothness and lack of variety, but the humor is frequently very expressive. As in Parny and Voltaire, the "vulgar" subject is actually a "high" subject turned inside out: the conception of Christ—a new twist, in Russian literature, at least. The several personal digressions by the poet have a fine lyric quality: most notable, probably, is the close, which looks forward, ironically and poignantly, to the poet's later marriage to Natalya Goncharova, the great beauty whose fickleness was to cost the poet his life in the duel with d'Anthès. Also eloquent is Satan's account of how he introduced Adam and Eve to the art of love. But essentially the *Gavriili-*

ada represents a blind alley in Pushkin's creation, and it had little if any influence on his subsequent work. In his later comic poems he was to discard the classic, rather hackneyed kind of travesty it represented in favor of a new blend of the mock-heroic with the everyday, the trivial but picturesque, and this mixture, also found in many passages of his master-piece, *Eugene Onegin*, was far closer to his unique talents and demonstrates greater integrity and conviction.

Unlike most of Pushkin's verse (except for his plays), the *Gavriiliada* is cast in iambic pentameter, with a constantly shifting rhyme scheme. This choice of verse, which Pushkin had scarcely yet mastered, also helps to account for the ex-cessive smoothness of the poem. In "Count Nulin" Pushkin employed his favorite meter, the iambic tetrameter, also with shifting rhyme scheme, and the shorter and more vigorous rhythm goes much better with the frequently colloquial tone of that poem. "The Little House in Kolomna" sees a return to pentameter, but at a time when Pushkin was far more practiced in that meter, and in the special poetic form of the octave.

Critics have pointed to Pushkin's youthful, unfinished poem, "The Monk," as the rhythmic prototype of the *Gav-riiliada*. Not only are the meter and the shifting rhyme scheme the same, but the language and tone of the early poem, written apparently when Pushkin was only fourteen, are surprisingly like the *Gavriiliada*. "The Monk," too, is a burlesque, based on an Old Russian comic anecdote about a hermit tempted by a demon, which appears to him in the guise of a beautiful woman. And like the *Gavriiliada*, it con-tains personal digressions and the would-be erotic "reminis-cences" of a young boy.

The relatively long verse line of the *Gavriiliada* has made it possible for me to adhere to the shifting rhyme scheme of the original very closely, and I have everywhere rhymed the same lines as the original and kept the distinction between masculine and feminine rhymes. In one case only (line 330 of the original) have I omitted a line which would have taken the third rhyme of a triple series; as a result my translation is one line shorter than Pushkin's original (as we have it in the

21

Tomashevski and Academia editions), and comparisons with the Russian after line 329 will require an adjustment of one line. It is hoped that the English reader can judge for himself how much of the humorous and expressive role is played by the rhymes.

GAVRIILIADA

(The Epic of Gabriel)

In truth, one Jewish maid I do revere
And cherish dear her pretty soul's salvation.
O come, angelic maid without a peer,
And take from me your peaceful consecration!
5   For I would save a child so ravishing:
By smile of honeyed lips intoxicated,
To our Lord Christ, the highest Heaven's King,
I sing my verses, chaste and consecrated.
The churchly airs may charm her with their art,
10   As she their humble music lies attending,
The Holy Ghost into her soul descending,
To capture so her inmost mind and heart.
      She's but sixteen, an innocent creation,
Dark-browed, a charming blouse where underneath
15   Two maiden hillocks make firm undulation;
Legs formed for love, a row of pearly teeth.
But why, my Jewess, is your gaze so fiery,
And why has such a glow spread o'er your cheek?
No, no, my dear, you've got it wrong entirely:
20   'Twas not of you—of Mary did I speak.
      Far from Jerusalem, the place neglected,
Away from urban sport and wastrel's joy,
Which Satan made that man he might destroy,
A beauty dwelt whose presence none suspected;
25   Without demanding much she lived her life.
A worthy man there chose her for his wife,
A gray-haired ancient but no shirker,
A carpenter, the village's sole worker.
Both day and nighttime, having much to do,
30   With trusty saw and level he created,
Thus busied, he had little time to view
The lovely maiden whom he scarcely knew,
That hidden flower for whose joy 'twas fated

23

High Heaven a greater honor should bestow;
35   Till then no man that flower e'er should know.
Nor did her husband ever think to water
That flower, lest it wilt in heat of day,
But he preferrred to treat her as a daughter,
And fed and clothed her—and kept far away.
40   Now, brothers mine, just at that very hour
Almighty God from Heaven's height discerned
That virgin figure, lovely in her bower,
And all at once with lust for her He burned.
In His unbounded wisdom He elected
45   That vineyard rich with promise now to bless
(That vineyard which till then had been neglected),
With His divine and bountiful largesse.
      But now the silent night its watch is keeping,
And in her corner Mary's sweetly sleeping.
50   Then God commands that she should
                                    dream that night:
Before her gaze there opens Heaven's height:
There endless vistas lie revealed in glory,
Spread over that refulgent territory;
Angelic choirs move on with stir and sweep,
55   And countless hordes of seraphim are flying,
As on their harpstrings cherubim are vying,
While grave archangels their deep silence keep
Within the cope of azure wings uplifted.
Now through the clouds that round-
                                    about have drifted
60   The throne of God in lightning splendor reared,
And blazing bright the face of God appeared...
All fell prostrate and Him in dread revered.
She bent her head, a proper awe displaying,
And trembled like a leaf as God was saying:
65   "Thou, earthly daughter, art beyond compare,
The hope of Israel; 'tis thy glad duty
To come to Me, enraptured by thy beauty,
Along with Me My godhead high to share.
Prepare thyself for all My ardor fervent:
70   The Bridegroom comes, He comes unto His servant!"

Again the face of God was veiled in clouds,
As wingèd angels swarmed about in crowds,
There sounded sweet the choirs of heavenly psalter...
Her hands she folded, facing Heaven's altar,
75   And opened wide her lips so roseate;
But what can so excite and agitate
Those youthful courtly looks of passion?
And who in all that crowd of popinjays
Is he who cannot take from her his gaze?
80   His plumèd helmet, his rich garb of fashion,
His azure wings and golden ringlets' blaze,
A figure tall, a look so unpresuming,
All this she liked, herself so unassuming.
So he alone from all of Heaven's crowd
85   Has pleased her—Angel Gabriel, be proud!
But now he's gone—the scene has vanished—
So pictures disappear when they are banished,
Extinguished on a magic lantern screen.
       So Mary woke from sleep: a dream she'd seen,
90   But dallied yet a while before it vanished.
For strange that dream, and to sweet Gabriel
Her mind was loath to bid a sad farewell.
To please the King of Heaven she was ready,
His words quite fresh and charming to her seemed,
95   And she had come to like Him well already—
But Gabriel the fairer one she deemed...
So often chance will turn infatuated
The marshal's lady and the aide-de-camp.
What can we do? All will say, 'twas fated,
100   The pedant just as surely as the scamp.
       But let's converse about love's stranger whims;
I have no mind for other conversation.
For at those times when at its excitation
We feel the blood course hot within our limbs,
105   And when the griefs of unrequited longing
Do vex us and encumber us with care,
Exhaust us and pursue us everywhere,
Then, our sorrows and our sufferings but prolonging,
We turn in anguish to seek out some friend

25

110   As confidant to lend us consolation,
Whose fervent speech of love with ours shall blend:
Translated, 'tis the speech of exultation.
And when, luck changing, we have caught in flight
A fleeting moment of intoxication,
115   And have inclined to blissful consummation
Some bashful beauty our love to requite,
And when we have forgot our past dejection
And of desire at last we see the end,
Why not relive it all in recollection,
120   In gossip with some confidential friend?
        And Thou, O God, hast known her agitation,
And Thou, like us, O Lord, with fire hast burned!
Thus e'en the Lord grew weary of creation,
And, bored by all the heavenly supplication,
125   To penning fervent psalms of love He turned:
" 'Tis Mary who's My love, " composed He,
"Immortal life's a burden I would fly;
Where are My wings?... With Mary I would lie,
And on her maiden's bosom now repose Me."
130   And so forth... He liked an Eastern style for verse,
And hence the lines He wrote were none too terse.
Then, calling Gabriel in consultation,
His passion He described to him in prose.
The Church has not revealed their conversation,
135   Which no Evangelist would e'er disclose,
But there's an old Armenian tradition
Which tells how God, Who had of show a dread,
Did choose an angel for the trip instead,
Perceiving he'd both wit and erudition,
140   And sent him out at eventime ahead.
The angel was displeased with such a mission,
Delivering letters struck him as too drear;
Recalling many a tedious expedition,
He rather looked to better his career.
145   Dissembling though, he strove to persevere,
And so the son of glory served as lurer
For Heaven's King—some would say procurer.
        But Satan never blinks an eye in rest!

He roamed the world, man's age-old adversary,
150 And learned that God was paying court to Mary,
That beauty whom His choice had richly blest
To save mankind from Hades' cruel damnation;
The news brought Satan very great vexation.
Above, meanwhile, the Lord was quite distraught,
155 And had a melancholy look about Him,
And though to rule the world He quite forgot,
All followed its accustomed way without Him.
But what is Mary up to? Where does she keep,
She who is Joseph's unfrequented treasure?
160 Alone and in her garden, near to sleep,
She spends an hour or two in guiltless leisure,
As poignant thoughts bring her almost to weep,
She dwells in memory on each handsome feature,
And would to Gabriel soar, a loving creature...
165 Beside a babbling brook, in palm tree's shade,
Her mind in loving meditation strayed.
She cared not for the perfumes of the flowers,
Nor for the gurgling sound that filled the hours...
But look: o'er her a handsome serpent swayed,
170 Its brilliant scales, seductive-looking, shining,
As through the boughs above her it kept twining,
And said to her, "O Heaven-favored lass,
I come to serve you—so be not heartless!"
'Tis possible? Oh, what has come to pass!
175 Whoe'er could say such things to one so artless!
Who could it be? It was the fiend, alas!
        The serpent's beauty, color in rich measure,
His greeting, eyes so full of cunning fire—
All this our maiden must perforce admire.
180 To wile away the tedium of leisure,
She turns to him the gaze of tender eyes
And starts the risky chat in such a wise:
"Who are you? Judging by your flattery,
Your beauty, brilliance, and your eyes' expression,
185 'Twas you revealed to Eve the mystery:
The place where to discover Eden's tree,
And there inspired her to work transgression.

27

The artless girl you brought to infamy,
And with her Adam's race and us enslaved.
190   In the abyss of sin we're vainly dying.
Aren't you ashamed?"
               "The preachers have been lying.
I did not ruin her, in truth, but saved."
"Saved! From whom?"
             "From God."
                    "A dangerous foe!"
"He was in love."
             "Take heed now! Have a care!"
195   "He burned for her..."
             "Be silent!"
                    "...with passion's glow."
Now Mary saw that it was touch and go.
"You're lying, snake!"
"God's truth!"
"Don't swear!"
"But hear me out!"
        She paused in hesitation:
"Can it be safe to sit here all alone
200   And listen to the snake's prevarication?
And should my silence its advice condone?
But Heaven's King has promised to protect me,
The Lord is merciful: He'll not reject me,
And for a trifle! For a harmless chat!
205   He surely won't expose His child to danger;
Besides, what mild and peaceful looks this stranger
Wears. What nonsense! Where's the harm in that?"
Thus she reflected, his vile suit abetting,
And thus of love and Gabriel forgetting.
210   The cunning serpent, uncoiling with *hauteur*
Its rattling tail, now curved its head around
To slide from off the twigs onto the ground,
In Mary's breast her passion to bestir.
He said to her: "With Moses' stiff narration
215   My tale does not at every point agree:
He won the Jews with lying information.
He played them false—and they refused to see.

28

God recompensed his intellect Nestorian
And made of him a ruler of great fame,
220 But I—believe me—am no court historian;
I covet not the prophet's sacred name.
     "They must—I mean, those many other beauties,
Be envious of your fiery eyes, indeed.
For you were born, O maid, for other duties,
225 To win the wonder of old Adam's breed,
To be the queen of their exultant gladness,
Rewarding their devotion with a smile.
To drive them with a word or two to madness,
To love them or not love them all the while...
230 Such is your lot. Like you, young Eve was weary,
Reposing in her garden, chaste and wise,
But innocent of love in Paradise,
Eternal tete-à-tetes with him were dreary,
There on the banks of Eden's shining stream,
235 Where they still lived a guiltless dream.
The tedium of endless days thus idle,
When neither leisure, youth, nor woodland idyll
Could kindle feeling in her maiden heart,
They passed together, strolling, eating, drinking,
240 By daytime yawning—at nighttime never thinking
To wile away the hours with passion's art...
What would you say? A tyrant overzealous
The Hebrew God, gloomy and jealous,
For, harboring desire for Adam's mate,
245 He kept her for Himself, the reprobate.
What honor's that? Where's the delectation,
When Heaven's not unlike incarceration?
Sit at His feet and pray in endless praise,
And flatter His esteem with courtly phrase;
250 Not dare to steal a look at any other;
Fond Gabriel treat only as a brother:
That is the lot, by God's own grand design,
Of any girl He takes as concubine.
And then what? Too soon you'll find displeasing
255 Your whole reward—the hoary cantor's wheezing,
Old women who their endless prayers orate,

The icons, candles, and the stuffy censing,
As deacons go about God's grace dispensing...
How merry! What an enviable fate!
260   "And so, my helpless pretty Eve befriending,
I took upon myself our Lord to vex
And put to Eve's and Adam's sleep an ending.
You've heard, no doubt, the things
                that happened next?
Two apples plucked from Eden's Tree of Knowing,
265 Where, tokens of love's power, they were growing,
Revealing to her gaze a fantasy
Of yet unfelt, unrealized inclinations,
Of her own face and figure's brilliancy:
The bliss of feeling, and heart's palpitations,
270 And Adam's young resplendent nudity.
I saw them both! And love—for that's my science—
On earth had thus inauguration fair:
Into the silent woodland strolled my pair,
And lay embracing there in fond alliance...
275 As to his wife's enticing thighs he clung,
Preoccupied, inept, devoid of tongue,
He sought the bliss of love's intoxication,
Consumed with reckless and devouring fire,
He strove to reach that fount of sweet sensation,
280 And, finding it, forgot all but desire...
And with him, all disheveled, Eve was lying,
Her passion God's vindictive wrath defying,
For there, her lovely mouth lightly inclining,
She kissed her husband's mouth with lips so red,
285 Wept tears of fondness, swooning in her bed,
And so they lay 'neath shade of palms reclining,
While Earth their trysting couch with flowers spread.
    "O blissful day! The newly wedded pair
Embraced from morn till night, their vigil keeping:
290 For well they knew it was no time for sleeping,
And how dawn's rising caught them unaware,
You know. The Lord, soon as He spied them,
From Paradise's meadows ostracized them.
He drove them out of Eden's garden blest,

295   Where all their hours were occupied with pleasure,
        And given over to the sweetest leisure,
        To the embraces of contented rest.
        But I revealed to them love's dark employments,
        The rights of spirited, light-hearted youth;
300   I showed them passion's secretest enjoyments:
        Embraces, raptures, love's tormenting truth.
        Tell me, I ask, can I have been a traitor?
        Have I to Adam's joy brought such sad end?
        But Eve, at least, still treats me as a friend,
305   I who was once her passion's liberator."
             The fiend fell silent. Mary all the while
        Lent ear without dissent to Satan's guile.
        "Perhaps," she thought, "it's not quite all a story:
        I've often heard that neither gold nor glory
310   Will serve to bring one any joy at all.
        Instead it seems that one in love must fall...
        In love! But how? For what? And what is needed?
        But as she listened to the fiend she heeded
        His story well, perceived its pregnant drift:
315   The actions, reasons strange, transports of passion,
        The daring style, the quest for a new fashion,
        Love's rapture and of lust the doubtful gift.
        Their cryptic import slowly gains coherence,
        As she gives in to fantasies unwise.
320   But suddenly she marks his disappearance:
        The snake is gone—or is it some disguise?
        She sees a handsome gallant there before her,
        Who at her feet is eager to adore her,
        And on her fixes his bewitching eyes.
325   With eloquence he begs to share her bower,
        One arm extends to her a pretty flower,
        But how his other arm doth disarrange
        Her robe, beneath which probes his eager finger
        In search of secrets where it fain would linger.
330   All this for Mary seems so new and strange.
        And at his touch a bold immodest blushing
        On maiden cheeks is amply manifest:
        A burning fever and a sigh come rushing

To stir within and raise her youthful breast.
335 She answers not; so crumble her defences,
And toward the fiend she bends her willing lips,
Her eyes closed fast, delight pervades her senses,
She cries alack! as on the grass she slips.
My love! To you were given o'er, in truth,
340 My childhood dreams of hope and sweet affection!
Beloved mistress of my gilded youth,
Will you forgive my painful recollection?
My sins, the sport of youth's depravity,
Those evenings spent amidst your family,
345 Your mother, tedious and exacting,
And how I bothered you, e'er distracting,
Endeavoring you to rouse from maiden sleep?
I taught your willing hand its new vocation
Of surrogate through our long separation,
350 The silent hours' vigil ever to keep,
And so console your sleepless agitation.
But faded is your youth now many a year,
The smile from your pale lips entirely vanished,
Time's ravages your beauty now have banished,
355 Can you forgive me all my sins, my dear?
O Hell's dark king, defiler of Mary's name!
You rose and took advantage of the maiden:
To you 'twas fair to see her heavy laden
With sin, as you her passion did inflame,
360 Corrupting thus the King of Heaven's bride,
And glad to see her virtue mortified.
So boast then, boast of your accursèd fame!
And seize your prize; but now the hour is near,
For twilight's gone and darkest night is here.
365 All's still. But suddenly toward prostrate Mary
There flew the angel, Heaven's legionary:
Love's envoy, Gabriel, intervened.
In horror at his look so painful,
Our beauty hid her visage shameful,
370 Disgruntled and uneasy rose the fiend,
And on his feet he said, "O haughty minion
From Heaven's ethereal courts, who bade you here,

32

And why have you deserted Heaven's sphere,
Why meddle thus in what is my dominion:
375   The pleasures of our fiendish regiments?"
But Gabriel gave answer, stern and frowning,
To Satan's questions, impudent and clowning:
"O maddened foe of Heaven's excellence,
Base villain, rascal, desperate pariah,
380   You've stained the honor of our sweet Maria—
Must I your brazen questionings now hear?
Be off at once, perpetual Denier,
Or I shall straightway make you quake with fear!"
"Ne'er have I quaked at sight of Heaven's legions,
385   God's cohorts which defend the upper regions,
Pimps, lackeys, whores, vile minions of the King,"
Thus baleful did the devil's answer ring.
Biting his lips, his somber forehead crinkling,
He whacked the angel's visage in a twinkling.
390   A cry resounded, Gabriel reeled back
Onto the ground, as his left knee went slack;
But suddenly he rose, filled with new ardor,
Biffed Satan on the temple all the harder
With blows quite unexpected. The devil bawled;
395   And then they rushed to interlock embraces,
But neither could prevail, though much they brawled:
Enchained thuswise, they roamed the open spaces,
Each raking his foe's bosom with his chin,
The other's legs in criss-cross fashion twisting,
400   The other's strength by strength and art resisting,
Each striving for himself the palm to win.
        Was it not thus? You all recall the pleasure,
When, comrades of my golden youth, in spring,
Deserting study, we would run at leisure
405   And make the meadows with our boy-
                        ish combat ring?
Thus tired, eschewing oaths and empty speech,
The angels, struggling, to each other cling.
Hell's brawling king, strong-thewed, with giant reach
Strains hard his slippery foe to overwhelm,
410   And now resolving to curtail their duel,

33

With one great blow strikes off his plumèd helm,
That golden helm, inset with many a jewel;
And seizing Gabriel by his soft hair,
He tugs him hard to set him sprawling
415   On the damp earth. Our Mary views their brawling,
Beholds the angel there, so young, so fair,
And for his safety she in silence shivers.
The devil's gaining; jubilant, Hell quivers,
But luckily the cunning Gabriel
420   Found with his teeth a spot quite unprotected—
That weapon which in battle is neglected—
The very member through which Satan fell.
Again he sank, the fiend! And off to Hell
He hardly made his way in deep vexation.
425   At that mad duel, that fearful altercation
Our beauty looked, scarce breathing, all bedazed,
As to her, victory won, he turned his gaze,
So full of charming, innocent affection
That love's red color rose in her complexion,
430   And her young soul was filled with tender care.
Ah, never had Maria seemed so fair!
        He blushed, constrained by purposes contrary,
But words divine and chaste his thoughts expressed:
"Rejoice, be glad, thou blameless virgin Mary,
435   Love be thy lot, 'mongst women greatly blest.
And blessed be in proud maternal feeling:
Your son shall save the world and cast down Hell!...
But for the world I'll not from you conceal it:
I think the Father greatly blest as well!"
440   Before the maiden he was humbly kneeling,
As all the while her hand he soft caressed...
She dropped her gaze and sighed, contritely blushing,
As his sweet kiss he on her cheek impressed.
Confused, her cheek a fiery red, voice hushing,
445   She felt the touch of hand upon her breast.
"Release me!" Mary whispered softly, flushing,
But as his lubrick kisses first resound,
The maid's last moan of innocence is drowned.
        What could she do? How put off

God's suspicion?
450 But do not grieve, my beauties all so shrewd,
For you, Love's confidantes, can e'er delude.
You know, with all your woman's intuition,
How best deceive the bridegroom's scrutiny
As well as those more skilled to pay attention,
455 And on the heels of love's felicity
Devise a counterfeit for chaste abstention.
From mother wanton daughter learns the art
Of simulating modest disposition,
Pretended torments, and complete submission,
460 For on that fateful night she plays a part.
Next morning she recovers just a little,
Arises pale, scarce walks, her look's so poor!
Her husband's rapturous, her mother noncommittal,
And at the window knocks her old amour.
465 　　Now Gabriel toward Heaven's height ascended,
As with glad tidings his way home he wended.
God, restless, welcomed His commissionaire,
His diligence and promptness He commended,
And asked what news he brought Him.
　　　　　　　　　　　　"Have no care,
470 I told her." "What did she answer?"
　　　　　　　　　　　　　　"She consented."
God bent His head, in sign He was contented,
Rose from His throne, and with far-darting eyes
Dismissed His court, as Zeus sent off his servants
Whene'er his countless offspring he'd chastise.
475 But pagan gods no longer find observance:
Zeus is defunct—and we have grown more wise.
　　Consoled the while by vivid recollection,
Our Mary lay at home in her retreat,
Stretched out, reposing on the rumpled sheet,
480 Her spirit burned with tenderest affection,
As passion made her youthful bosom rise.
She called to Gabriel, her new-found lover,
To come and claim again the hidden prize,
With dextrous foot she put aside the cover,
485 While on her lips a blissful smile there hovered,

35

And, happy in her glorious nakedness,
Herself she marvelled at her loveliness!
But while she rests alone in meditation,
She sins no less, our beauteous libertine,
490   And drinks the cup of calm intoxication.
Her plight amuses you, you cunning fiend!
So while beside her window Mary's lying,
A feathery white-wingèd dove comes flying.
Above her now it flutters, now it flits.
495   Round and about it circles, gay hymn tunes singing,
And suddenly between her thighs awinging,
It comes to rest beneath her dress and sits,
Begins to peck her, fluttering and whirling,
The while its tiny feet and beak are twirling.
500   " 'Tis He! 'Tis He in truth!" Our Mary grasps
That in a pigeon's form she's now regaling
Another; screams and clasps her thighs; then paling,
Begins to tremble, supplicates and gasps;
Defeated, bursts in tears, cries out and shivers.
505   It coos, triumphant; joyfully it quivers.
But, spent at last and drawn to sleep, the dove
Now shades beneath its wing the Flower of Love.
     It flies away. Our maiden now feels weary
And muses thus: "Their pranks seem slightly dreary!
510   One, two, three—you'd think they'd
                     soon grow bored!
At all events—today I've not been lonely:
All three—the devil, Gabriel, the Lord—
In one short day all three of them have known me."
     The Almighty Lord consented—as was right—
515   To recognize the child as His descendant,
But Gabriel—O destiny resplendent!
Did not refrain from meeting her at night.
Like many husbands, Joseph too consented—
And lived with Mary chaste but quite contented.
520   He loved the infant as his own dear son,
For which from God a great reward he won.
     Amen, amen! How shall I end my story?
Forgetting faults that were but transitory,

O wingèd Gabriel, I sang thy fate:
525   To thee alone I vowed to dedicate
My humble lyre's fond canto of salvation:
Preserve me, angel, heed my supplication.
In love I've been a heretic till now,
Mad worshiper of many a heavenly beauty,
530   Scamp, demon's friend who spurned the
                                                voice of duty...
Accept today my heart's repentant vow!
My vices old I'll willingly surrender:
I've just seen Helen—for her I'll mend my ways,
For she's as sweet as Mary's heart is tender;
535   My soul will worship her for all my days!
Give to my speech the wit of fascination,
Teach me the secret: how to please her well,
Implant in her love's ardent inclination,
Or otherwise I'll go and pray to Hell!
540   But time runs on and age's silvery greying
Will soon encroach upon my sable head,
And then, in seriousness, my prospects weighing,
At last I'll choose some gentle maid to wed.
Then let me pray to thee, O saintly Joseph,
545   I beg of thee, bowed down on bended knee,
For thou the cuckolds' patron saint wert chosen,
I pray, withhold thy blessings not from me.
Grant me thy patience pious, thy endurance,
I pray, and ever down upon me send
550   Calm sleep and fairest dreams, thy own assurance,
Peace in my home, and trust in each good friend!

NOTES

Ll. 1-12. I apologize to the reader for this somewhat pretentious, heavy-handed and not always meaningful opening, but the style of this passage is rather faithful to the original in all these respects.

L. 1. The Jewish girl who is the object of this apostrophe is probably the daughter of a tavern keeper in Kishinev, where Pushkin was living when he wrote the *Gavriiliada*.

L. 12. Literally, "The master He of thoughts and hearts."

L. 17. Literally, "Why have you smiled?"

L. 27. Literally, "A grey-haired ancient, a bad carpenter and joiner."

Ll. 36-37. Literally, "Her lazy husband did not water it with his old watering-can in the morning hours."

L. 48. Literally, "Already the dumb night embraces the fields."

L. 62. Literally, "All fell face down... The sound of harps grew silent."

L. 78. Pushkin's "young courtiers," as he calls them, are perhaps not precisely "popinjays," but the anomalous reference is in the spirit of his humorous blasphemy.

L. 100. Literally, "The boor and the pedant agree in that."

L. 118. Literally, "And we have nothing more to expect."

Ll. 130-131. Literally, "And so forth... All that He could invent—The Creator liked a colorful Eastern style."

L. 135. Literally, "The Evangelist failed in this somewhat."

L. 136. The "old Armenian tradition" mentioned here has not been identified; Pushkin obviously knew one or more New Testament apocryphal tales about the Annunciation, but which ones and in what form is uncertain.

L. 142. Literally, "Not infrequently had he had the luck to serve as emissary," an irony that I have made more explicit.

Ll. 154-155. Literally, "And he [Satan] bustled about. Meanwhile, the Almighty sat in heaven in [sweet] melancholy."

L. 201. Literally, "And, anyway, should I put trust in Satan?"

L. 218. Literally, "Praise Him, wonder at His beauty."

L. 251. Literally, "Don't dare speak a quiet word to the Archangel [Gabriel]."

L. 258. Literally, "Painted [i.e., the icons] by some icon-dauber [*bogomaz*]."

L. 274. Literally, "There their glances and hands soon went astray..."

L. 301. Literally, "The kiss [I revealed to them], and tender words."

Ll. 304-305. Literally, "I think not! But I only know that I have remained Eve's friend."

Ll. 316-317. Literally, "The daring style, and the unrestrained images; we all are fond of something new."

L. 321. Literally, "And a new thing is before her."

Ll. 327-329. Literally, "The other crumples the simple linen cloth and steals hurriedly beneath her garments; a light finger playfully touches sweet secrets..." I have omitted one line here (l. 330 of the original), and thus suppressed a triple rhyme which would have rhymed with ll. 328 and 329.

38

L. 339. The identity of the young lady addressed here seems to be unknown.

Ll. 346-347. Literally, "I tormented you with a secret anxiety, and gave enlightenment to your innocent beauties." the word "beauty" (*krasa*), in the singular or plural, is often used in Russian poetry as a metonymic figure for the possessor of that beauty.

Ll. 358-359. The enjambment here is not in the original.

L. 387. Literally, "The accursed one spoke, and, burning with malice." The verb "spoke" (*rek*), an archaic Church Slavonicism, is used several times by Pushkin in this work.

L. 401. Literally, "Each seeks to pull the other after him."

Ll. 402-405. Pushkin is recollecting here his schoolboy days at the Lyceum at Tsarskoe Selo.

L. 409. Literally, "Vainly grunted with his slippery foe."

Ll. 423-424. Literally, "The accursed one fell! And begging mercy, he hardly found the way back to dark Hell."

L. 463. Literally, "Her husband's enraptured; her mother whispers, 'Thank God!' "

L. 471. Literally, "And the King of Heaven, saying not a word."

L. 483. Literally, "Preparing her secret gift for his love."

L. 495. Pushkin describes these tunes as "gay," but I have also made them "hymn tunes."

Ll. 501-502. The enjambment is my own addition.

L. 511. Literally, "I can say, I've had a lot of fuss."

L. 513. It is perhaps superfluous to point out that Mary's attitude is a clear case of psychological projection of her own mental state.

L. 530. Literally, "Demon's friend, scamp and betrayer."

L. 544. Both Tomashevski's edition of 1922 and the Academia edition of 1936 address this prayer to Gabriel as the "consoler of Joseph." But most of the early manuscript versions of the poem have the address to Joseph himself as the patron saint of cuckolds, and indeed this seems to make better sense.

COUNT NULIN

The comic poem "Count Nulin" was a product of that period of Pushkin's exile that he passed on his family estate of Mikhailovskoe, near Pskov in West Russia. He wrote the poem in a burst of inspiration on the two successive mornings of December 13 and 14, 1825.

The initial impulse for the poem ostensibly came from his reading of Shakespeare's "Rape of Lucrece." As Pushkin later put it when he recalled the poem's conception:

At the end of 1825 I was in the country. While reading "Lucrece," a rather weak poem by Shakespeare, I reflected: what if it had occurred to Lucretia to give Tarquin a slap?

Perhaps it would have had the effect of cooling off his resolution, and he would have been forced to retire shamefully from the field? Lucretia would then not have stabbed herself, Publicola would not have become enraged, Brutus would not have driven out the kings, and the world and its history would have been different. And so we owe the republic, the consuls, the dictators, the Catos, and Caesar to a titillating incident, not unlike one that recently took place in the vicinity here, in Novorzhevski District. The idea of parodying history and Shakespeare occurred to me; I could not resist the double temptation and in two days finished this tale.

In fact, there are notable points of contact with, and parody of, Shakespeare's poem, such as the feverish passion and trepidation that seize Tarquin as he contemplates the possibility of the act of rape. The comparison that likens Nulin, stealing down the corridor toward the lady's room, to a cat in pursuit of a mouse, may well derive from Shakespeare's simile comparing Tarquin, standing over Lucrece's head, to a "grim lion," fawning "o'er his prey." Pushkin underlined this element of parody in the poem's original title, "A modern Tarquin." In spite of his respect and admiration for Shakespeare (he had just completed his own chronicle play from Russian history, *Boris Godunov*, in a deliberate attempt to in-

41

troduce the beneficial influence of the Shakespearean theater to the Russian stage), Pushkin's healthy common sense and practical grasp of life and its realities must have made the poem's sentimental subject appear ridiculous to him. Tomashevski suggests that the poem was inspired by a reflection on the sense of history, a theme that had in fact preoccupied Pushkin in the writing of *Boris Godunov*. A few days before he wrote "Count Nulin," Pushkin heard from friends that the reigning tsar, Alexander I, the sovereign responsible for Pushkin's exile, was dead. Might Pushkin have not then reflected that such individual and seemingly chance events might alter the course of history irrevocably? And in fact, the death of Alexander and the subsequent crisis it produced for the succession (Alexander died without a son) triggered the Decembrist Uprising of liberal dissident nobles and did threaten for a short time to change the course of Russian history. (Just so the False Dmitri, appearing as if by chance, had taken the throne away from Boris Godunov and his son.)

Yet the real sense of "Count Nulin" is neither in a parody of Shakespeare nor a meditation, ironic or serious, on the course of history. The poem's parallels to Shakespeare are not many, and the parodic content relatively thin. It is a picture of a vivid (if static) contemporaneity, rather than a sense of historical development, that the poem gives us. The humor is more that of picturesque, vignette-like details from daily life on a country estate, than it is a humor of parody, or even of satire. The key phrase in Pushkin's statement quoted above is rather the reference he makes to "an incident, not unlike one that took place in the vicinity here." Imagination can readily conjure up a scene from real life quite similar to Nulin's frustrated escapade. Travelling accidents of the type portrayed were not infrequent, Russian landowners, bored on their isolated estates, hospitable, and the absence of a husband was hardly a rigid pretext for denial of the hospitality that class solidarity demanded. In actual fact, however, Pushkin is referring here to an incident that occurred not in 1825 but in 1829, to a friend of his who, in that year, recorded in his diary: "I paid a visit in the style of Count Nulin with this

42

his diary: "I paid a visit in the style of Count Nulin with this one difference, that I was not slapped."

The poem is infused with Pushkin's typical tongue-in-cheek irony, but here the humor of his customary ironic tone is overshadowed by the brilliant catalogue of details of country life. The contrast between the heroine's tedious novel of endless sentimental romance and the vivid picture of a September morning in the farmyard of a country estate is unforgettable: the yard fowl dragging through the mud, the fight between goat and dog, the laughing brats, the crone sloshing her way to hang up the wash on the fence—all this is probably closer to the imagination of a Gogol, with his ability to evoke the most trivial or grotesque details and endow them with life and vigor, than to Pushkin himself. And indeed, all the characters of the piece and their comedy are endowed with the Gogolian trait of *poshlost'*, that peculiarly Russian term and the vice it denotes—a trivial, dreary and common vulgarity and pettiness of spirit—a mood that Gogol evoked so memorably in his *Inspector-General* and *Dead Souls*. All three of Pushkin's principal characters share this quality of *poshlost'*, though each in a distinctly different way. And though Pushkin's humor of situation is more classically limned (and less comical) than Gogol's, still the central misunderstanding that sets the plot going in "Count Nulin" may be seen to anticipate Gogol's great comedies of situation based on the misapprehension of events.

Details are fundamental both to the realism and to the humor of "Count Nulin": the housewife's frenzied toilette in anticipation of Nulin's arrival, or the catalogue of articles Nulin carries with him in his trunk; the last-named object, though it lacks the mystery of Chichikov's trunk in *Dead Souls*, does function as a symbol of its master's character, so closely linked with its contents, and does, like Gogol's, have something of a life of its own. Nulin's carriage, compared in Gogolian style to a wounded living being, is another such symbol of its master. That these details should be funny depends on the tone of irony and lightness with which Pushkin has suffused the whole.

Curiously, it was this comedy of picturesque and frivolous details that was most misunderstood by critics and readers in Pushkin's day. "Count Nulin" was almost universally attacked for its triviality and vulgarity, and the critic Nadezhdin condemned it for the "worthlessness" of its subject and the "baseness" of the life depicted in it. Today we take the bathos of many of these details for granted; it will hardly make them seem any funnier for us if we reflect that this stratum of the poem was totally new to Russian readers of the 1820's, but it will illustrate for us the poem's essential originality in the developing context of Russian literature. The burlesque treatment of a vulgar subject in elevated terms was already familiar to Russian readers from Maykov's eighteenth-century mock-epic, *Yelisey*. But Pushkin's poem, a low treatment of low personages and events, did not correspond to any of the classic parodic types, while the realistic bathos of "Count Nulin" contrasted sharply to the idealizing Romanticism his contemporaries were coming to prefer in the mid-1820's.

There is also a good deal of satire in Pushkin's poem, the chief target of which is Russian Gallomania. Nulin himself, the "fop and popinjay," is its exponent, but the heroine too is not free from implicit criticism either. In the ethical plane of the work (if we can speak of it quite seriously) we see a pointed contrast between "French" frivolity and flirtatiousness and a healthy "Russian" virtue, common-sensical if a bit crude. A product of a French education and the reading of French novels, the heroine vacillates between the French and Russian types, but her native Russian nature asserts itself vigorously over the thin veneer of French breeding when Nulin upsets her *sang-froid*.

In satirizing Gallomania Pushkin continues a line begun in Russian literature by such earlier writers as Fonvizin and Krylov. Of course, Pushkin, who adored French classic literature, was not really anti-French. But he did deplore what he felt to be the decline of French taste in the transition from Classicism to Romanticism: Lamartine could not replace Parny in his esteem, nor Guizot Voltaire.

A good deal of the humor of the poem (in contrast to the *Gavriiliada* and in anticipation of "The Little House in

Kolomna") is bound up with the poetic form itself: the choice of rhymes and of meter. The rhyme words in "Count Nulin" are often vigorous and expressive, and foreign words (as in *Eugene Onegin*) are sometimes chosen for their humorous effect as rhymes. We may also cite the use of triple rhymes, and the ever shifting rhyme scheme, which recalls the *Gavriiliada*. In this poem Pushkin uses his more familiar and more vigorous iambic tetrameter, rather than the smoother, monotonous pentameter he had employed in the earlier poem. There are concessions to the colloquial, bathetic tone: frequent use of enjambment, and the practice of occasionally letting rhyming lines cross the section divisions. Though rhyme has an important semantic role in the poem (the rhyme words are often emphasized, or especially comic), it cannot be said that the rhyme patterns themselves are anything but arbitrary. Thus, at times Pushkin completes a rhyme pattern at the end of a section (which is normal), but at other times he lets it lap over into the next section. For this reason I have permitted myself a liberty I have not taken in either of the other two poems in this collection: I have altered the rhyme pattern to suit my own rhyming needs. This has greatly helped, I trust, in preserving the fresh, lively and frequently colloquial tone of the work. It must be added that I have preserved all the basic rhyme patterns in Pushkin (aabb, abab, abba, as well as longer patterns employing triple rhymes), and I have tried to alternate them somewhat as the poet does. I have also permitted myself the free alternation of masculine and feminine rhymes in this translation.

COUNT NULIN

(Count Nocount)

'Tis time, 'tis time! The horn resounds,
The grooms in hunting dress arrayed,
And straining at the leash the hounds—
All's ready since the break of day.
5   The master stands atop the stair,
His arms akimbo, to survey
The lively scene, with the solemn air
Of one who'll ride to the hounds today.
He sports a doublet for the ride,
10   With a Turkish dagger in his sash;
A flask of rum fast at his side,
Where hangs his horn on its chain of brass.
In nightcap from her room inside
His sleepy spouse espies the scene,
15   And glowers down with angry mien
At all that canine disarray.
Her husband, as they bring his steed,
Shouts up, "I won't be home today!"
Vaults on his horse with headlong speed;
20   The cavalcade is on its way!

During September's last few days
(Pray pardon the prosaic phrase!)
The country's dull; the weather's foul,
With autumn wind and rain for days,
25   And howl of wolves. But Nimrod sees
Advantage here, and spurning ease,
On fallow fields he will cavort
And bivouac; swear like a trooper,
Eat, drink himself into a stupor—
30   All in pursuit of manly sport.

What chores performs his wife at home,

Abandoned there and quite alone?
Don't fancy she'll have any peace;
Her tasks are set: to feed the geese,
35   Mushrooms to salt, meals to prepare;
Her sharp eye should be everywhere.
In barns and cellars she should spy
To see if anything's awry.

Our heroine, alas, instead
40   (But wait, the poor thing has no name!
"Natasha" 's what her husband said,
But let us use the form that's right:
"Natalya Pavlovna" we'll write.)
Natalya Pavlovna, the while,
45   Neglects her chores, for as a child
She never learned the household art;
Far from her paternal hearth
Our youthful heroine was bred—
To Madame Falbalà's she went,
50   A proper girls' establishment.

She sits now at the windowside,
And on her lap lies open wide
A novel—volume number five—
About two loves who correspond,
55   Fair Héloise, and her Armand.
A tedious, tedious compilation;
The story's classic and old-fashioned,
Composed without imagination,
Stiff, ethical and unimpassioned.

60   At first this dreary novel she
Takes up and reads attentively,
But soon her eyes begin to stray.
Outside there's matter more exciting:
The yard dog and the goat are fighting,
65   And so she turns to watch the fray,
While circling urchins squeal with laughter,
And melancholy turkeys gabble

47

And in the autumn rain run after
A solitary cock bedraggled.
70 Three puddle-paddling ducks immerse
Themselves. Across the yard goes sloshing
A crone to hang up all the washing.
The weather's slowly getting worse,
And snow is due at any time...
75 But hark! There sounds a bell's clear chime.

You know the country's isolation,
Dear friends, and understand full well
How hearts can beat in expectation,
Hearing the peal of carriage bell.
80 Is it a friend from far away,
Or comrade from one's old school days?...
Or... O my God! Can it be she?
Nearer it sounds, and nearer still.
And now in close proximity—
85 Then passes by.... And all is still.

Our heroine, enraptured, runs
Onto the balcony to look:
And there she sees, beyond the mill,
Across the stream a carriage comes.
90 It's on the bridge—it's drawing near—
But no, it's veering left. Mute, stunned,
She gazes, winking back a tear.

But see—the carriage turns too hard,
Tilts, sways and on its side it falls.
95 "There's been a crash! Run quick!" she bawls,
"And tow them here into the yard.
To dine with us invite the master.
But is he still alive?... Run faster!
Find out at once!"
                        The servant goes.
100 Swiftly she runs to put her clothes
In order, and fluff up her hair,
Throw on a shawl, draw up a chair,

48

The curtains close—then sit and wait...
At last they straggle through the gate.
105 Begrimed and filthy from long driving,
The carriage, hardly yet surviving,
Is pushed and dragged into the yard.
The youthful master hobbles slow,
While his French valet, named Picard,
110 Exhorts, *"Allons, courage*—let's go!"
They cross the porch, the entranceway;
Meanwhile a door is opened wide
Into a room that's set aside
For the young lord's impending stay.
115 Bustling and shuffling the man goes
To help his master change his clothes;
Let's seize this opportunity
To indicate who this can be:
Count Nulin, prodigal and spendthrift,
120 To Petersburg he's on his way
To play the fop and popinjay,
With haberdashery resplendent:
Of frock-coats, vests and shirts a pile,
All tailored in the latest style;
125 Hats, fans, capes, corsets, laces, stays,
Each calculated to amaze;
Pins, collar studs, and hose *à jour*,
Guizot's alarming new brochure;
Of colored handkerchiefs a lot,
130 The latest thing by Walter Scott;
Parisian *mots* he'd found hilarious,
And Beranger's most recent song;
Bits taken from Italian arias—
This catalogue is much too long.

135 All's set; the time for dinner nears,
Below the mistress waits impatient.
At last her visitor appears.
She makes polite interrogation:
What of his leg? Is he in pain?
140 Count Nulin, quieting her fears,

Replies, "Not bad; I can't complain!"
Thus chatting, they sit down to eat:
Closer to her he moves his seat.
His talk consists of loud abuse
145   At the expense of Mother Rus.
We Russians hibernate, he rants,
Far from the sunny joys of France.
"But how's the theatre?" "Ah, the stage!
C'est bien mauvais, ça fait pitié.
150   For Talma's much too frail to play,
And Mamselle Mars, alas, has aged.
Of course there is *le grand Potier!*
His is the only famous name
That still retains its old allure."
155   "What writers now have come to fame?"
"There's Lamartine and d'Arlincourt."
"We Russians imitate them too."

"No, really now! That's something new!"
Can it then be, despite our past,
160   That we'll be civilized at last!"
"How do they wear their gowns?" "Quite low,
Down to the very... this far, so.
But let me look at *you* awhile;
Indeed... the cut, the ruches, bows
165   Are very close to the new style."
"We take the *Moscow Telegraph*."
"Ah, would you enjoy a laugh?
A vaudeville tune?" Without ado
The gallant count begins to sing.
170   "But Count, you've eaten scarce a thing!"
"I'm full, it seems." "Well then." The two
Arise. The young and pretty wife
Is in a most vivacious mood;
The count, forgetting Paris life,
175   Shows a surprised solicitude.
The evening slips, unnoticed, by,
The count's distracted, and her eye
Now shines so radiantly clear,

Now droops, so diffident and shy.
180 Before they know it, midnight's here.
The lackey in the hallway snores;
The cock crows loudly out of doors,
Where the nightwatchman makes his round;
The candles gutter and burn low,
185 The lady to her bed will go,
Bidding her guest, "Good-night, sleep sound!"
The count arises in vexation
And, filled with tender expectation,
Kisses her hand. Our heroine,
190 Inspired by a desire to please—
Dear God! forgive this flirt her sin—
Now gives his hand a stealthy squeeze.

Natalya Pavlovna's undressed;
In front of her Parasha stands.
195 (Parasha is her stewardess
And confidante of all her plans.)
She mongers news, she knits, she sews,
She begs from all their worn-out clothes.
She's quick to joke with her young master—
200 Gets angry at him even faster—
And to her mistress boldly lies.
Just now she ventures to advise
Her mistress all about the count,
Omitting naught from her account;
205 God knows from where she heard the stuff.
Her mistress answers with a frown:
"You're boring me to tears. Enough!"
She dons her nightcap and her gown,
Turns out Parasha, and lies down.

210 And as she's laying down her head,
The count too's getting into bed,
But first he calls for a cigar;
No sooner said, than 'Sieur Picard
Produces one—plus other things:
215 Wine, tweezers fitted out with springs,

A lamp, a clock, nor's he forgot
That novel by Sir Walter Scott.

At last reclining in his bed,
The count endeavors now to read;
220   Alas! Tonight he'll not succeed!
For nibbling notions in his head
Are nagging him. Can it be true
That he's in love? Here's something new!
How droll, and just a bit unlikely,
225   And yet a noble thing. No doubt
About it: she surely likes me,
He thinks and snuffs the candle out.

A fever dread he can't resist
Has come to frustrate his sound sleep.
230   Ah! Satan's busy: thoughts illicit
Swarm in his brain. He cannot keep
From thinking of that gaze which he
Found eloquent yet womanly,
Remembering her ripe perfection:
235   Her swelling forms, replete, well fed,
The country glow of her complexion,
Redder than any rouge is red.
He calls to mind her foot so slender
And how with casual touch and tender
240   Her hand had come to squeeze his hand.
How could he, fool, misunderstand?
Right then he should have seized his chance
And used that moment to advance;
Still there's no need to think he's balked:
245   Her chamber door's no doubt unlocked.
Donning his silken dressing-gown,
He presses forward in the dark
While knocking chairs and footstools down.
Like Tarquin dressed in modern garb
250   All risk and scandal he defies
In his fond quest of passion's prize.

52

Just as the cunning cat at play,
The pampered pet of the servants' hall,
Picking a mouse for its just prey,
255   Now creeps along with stealthy crawl.
Now slinks, half screwing up its eyes,
With archèd back and lashing tail;
Unsheathes its claws to seize the prize,
Then pounce! the victim's fast impaled.

260   Th'enamoured Nulin in the gloom
Lurches and gropes across the room,
Impelled by passion's fatal heat;
His breathing's tight, his tread's constrained:
He trembles lest beneath his feet
265   The floor should creak. Now he's attained
The Heavenly Gate. He tries the catch
And presses lightly on the latch;
It gently yields without a sound;
He looks: the lamp, though burning low,
270   Bathes the pale bedroom in its glow;
But is the lady sleeping sound,
Or feigning sleep? He cannot know.

Afraid to advance, loath to retreat
He quails—and tumbles at her feet.
275   And she... But now, with their permission,
My lady readers I entreat
To comprehend her dire position
And keep her perilous plight in view;
Please counsel me: what should she do?

280   Waking she opens wide her eyes
And sees the count. On bended knee
Her charms he seeks to eulogize,
And with a hand he shamelessly
Essays to touch her comforter
285   (A move that does not comfort her).
But casting off all hesitation

53

And spurred by righteous indignation,
And... could it be?... a touch of fear,
She boxes noble Tarquin's ear.
290   A magisterial slap, in truth!
A slap, and what a slap, forsooth!

The count is staggered by the blow:
To suffer such humiliation!
With mind enflamed with blind vexation,
295   To what extremes will he not go?
Just then a yapping lapdog's bark
Rouses Parasha; through the dark
She comes (the count can hear her tread!).
And, cursing fate for his sad plight,
300   And damning women's wilfulness,
He takes to his heels in craven flight.

Now if the reader can conceive
The stir that night, the sleeplessness,
Th'ensuing row—you have my leave!
305   For none of this will I discuss.

Next day arising silently,
Count Nocount's mien is pale, depressed.
He pares, distraught and listlessly,
His rosy nails, yawns, starts to dress.
310   He ties his tie with languid air,
And though he wets his fine-toothed comb,
He cannot put it to his hair.
His deepest thoughts? All, all unknown!
His plans? 'Tis plain: he must erase
315   That look of sullen rage and shame,
So down he goes.

                    The fair scapegrace,
Biting her lips, essays to hide
The mocking glance, the look of blame,
She turns the breakfast conversation
320   To this, to that. First mortified,

But shedding soon all trepidation,
The count gives answer with a smile.
And lo! within a little while
He's making jests—and good jests, too,
325 Prepared to fall in love anew.
A noise outside. Who can it be?
"Hello, my dear." "My God, it's he!
Count, meet my husband!" Then, "My dear,
This is Count Nulin." "How d'ye do!
330 What frightful weather! But I hear
Your carriage now has been repaired.
It's at the smithy, good as new.
My dear, down by the garden plot
The hunting dogs ran down a hare.
335 Hey, vodka! Count, you'll have a spot,
This is good stuff—you can't resist!
And so you'll stay with us and dine?"
"Well, no—you see, I'm rather pressed."
"Oh, come, my wife and I insist!
340 You know, we're awfully glad of guests—
Please stay!" But, partly from vexation,
And newly blighted expectation,
The count is strongly disinclined.
Downing a stiff one for the road,
345 Picard's soon reeling with the load
Of baggage he lugs down. Two men
Bring out the trunk and bolt it down.
Now all is ready for the ride;
Picard jams everything inside,
350 And off they go... Thus our tale ends,
Or so at least it should, my friends;
But let me add a word or two.

The carriage had scarce flashed from view
Than the young husband's heard about
355 Nocount's assault and shameful rout.
(She told the tale to neighbors too.)
And which of all her confidants
Laughed longest at the history?

55

You'll never guess! "Give me a chance:
360 Her husband then?" —Oh, no, not he!
His righteous anger knew no bound,
He said that Nulin was a fool,
A milksop; if he came around
He'd take his dogs and run him down,
365 And then you'd hear him whine and pule!
No, 'twas *Lidin* laughed, you see,
A nearby squire of twenty-three...

If ancient times we can compare
To ours, I must in truth disclose
370 That faithful wives are not so rare
As you, my friends, might have supposed.

NOTES

Title. The name Nulin is derived from Russian *nul'* ("zero"), suggesting the possibility of a pun in the English ("Count Nocount") that has no model in the Russian title (*"Graf Nulin"*).

Ll. 7-8. Literally, "His self-satisfied face shines with a pleasant seriousness," a description that implies something more permanent concerning the husband's character than my rendering does.

L. 9. The "doublet" is actually a *chekmen'*, a short wool coat or caftan of Caucasian type. Pushkin was fond of exotic costumes, especially for riding, and often affected them.

L. 21. This passage, as well as some of the descriptive passages that follow, reflect the tedium of Pushkin's enforced stay on the Mikhailovskoe estate.

L. 22. Literally, "speaking in despised prose," a typical literary irony of Pushkin's that calls attention to the bathetic character and style of much of the poem.

L. 23. This line does not rhyme in my translation, but the reader should note that Pushkin himself has failed to rhyme one line near the end of the poem (corresponding to line 369 of this translation).

Ll. 27-30. Pushkin has another humorous image here, that of a devastating raid the hunter carries out against the wasteland, but I have found it easier to develop the implicit ironic contradiction Pushkin gives of self-deprivation for the sake of sport.

Ll. 31-32. Here Pushkin rhymes *supruga* ("spouse," feminine nominative singular) with *supruga* ("spouse," masculine genitive singular); the example is celebrated in the history of Russian rhyme as an instance where two distinct derivatives of the same root which happen to coincide phonetically are rhymed. Still the rhyme is not really quite successful. I have abandoned the idea of rhyming "spouse" with "spouse" as too flat, but perhaps it is worth pointing out that in lines 83 and 85 I have rhymed the word "still" in different senses, and in ll. 258 and 261 the word "sound," also in different meanings.

L. 35. It should be pointed out that the typical landowner's wife conjured up in this passage does not actually have to cook the meals, but only plan and order them.

L. 40. This line does not rhyme in my translation.

Ll. 40-44. Pushkin never rhymes the name Natalya Pavlovna, since the two names have no rhyming counterpart. Natasha, the nickname derived from Natalya, can appear alone and does rhyme in Russian, though not, alas, in English.

L. 50. Falbala, a playful French name (it means "furbelow"); Pushkin calls her an "immigrant."

L. 53. Actually it is volume number four, but the rhymes offered by "four" provided no help.

Apparently no one has established whether the reference here is to an actual French novel of the period or to an imaginary one, and my own efforts to determine this likewise failed. The vogue of the epistolary novel continued well into the nineteenth century. It may seem unlikely that a reader of such fiction would have shown the literary sophistication that the heroine later demonstrates in line

57

157.

Ll. 58-59. Literally, "moral and dignified, lacking in romantic intrigues."

L. 60. Pushkin repeats the name and patronymic of his heroine here, but these occupy a total of six of the line's eight syllables and greatly cramp the choice of rhymes.

L. 63. This comment has been invented by me, since the content of two Russian lines naturally compressed to one in English (line 64).

Ll. 70-71. The enjambment here is my addition.

Ll. 76-85. This digression is highly personal, recalling again the tedium of Pushkin's stay at Mikhailovskoe in 1824-1826. Two school friends, Pushchin and Delvig, had indeed visited him there in spite of the political risk their visits entailed. The "she" of line 82 is Mme. A.P. Kern, the celebrated beauty who inspired Pushkin's famous lyric, "I Remember a Wonderful Moment."

L. 87. This line does not rhyme in my translation.

Ll. 93-96. In this passage I have had to sacrifice the heroine's involuntary cry of "O joy!" as well as the nicknames of the two house servants, Fil'ka and Vas'ka, since neither of these names could provide a rhyme.

Ll. 105-106. Pushkin describes the carriage as "seriously wounded"; I have at least retained the conceit that it is an animate being, with the rhyme word "surviving."

L. 109. I introduce Picard's name six lines earlier than Pushkin does, for the sake of the rhyme with "yard."

L. 110. Pushkin's Picard of course speaks French and says only, "Allons, courage!"; the latter word rhymes with *ekipazh* (carriage), but I was unable to use the rhyme; nor could I rhyme "Allons!" Perhaps there is some humor in having Picard mix French and English in macaronic fashion.

Ll. 115-116. Picard's "shuffling" (literally, "rustling") and "bustling" is presumably directed toward carrying luggage, rather than helping his master change clothes.

Ll. 119-134. On the name Nulin, see the note on the title. This name does not serve for any rhymes in the original, and I have refrained from the obvious temptation to rhyme it with such words as "fooling." Pushkin tells us that Nulin is coming from "abroad" (France), where he "had dissipated his future revenues"; he is on his way to Petersburg to "be shown off, like some strange beast." Of all this I have managed to retain only the epithets of "spendthrift" and "popinjay" (both of which have yielded rhymes); I have been more successful in the catalogue of Nulin's wardrobe and luggage: from the long list Pushkin gives nothing has been changed, and I have had to sacrifice only "lorgnettes" and "an album of malicious caricatures."

L. 127. Hose *à jour* are hemstitched stockings.

L. 128. Francois Pierre Guillaume Guizot (1787-1874), French statesman and historian, noted for his somewhat liberal views and his criticism of the Bourbons after their restoration, as well as for his famous advice to any and all, "Enrichissez-vous!" He supported Louis Philippe in the July, 1830 Revolution and was made minister. I take it from Pushkin's use of the diminutive form *knizhka* that he has one of Guizot's many pamphlets in mind, and not his major treatises, some in a number of volumes; in a letter of this period to his brother, Pushkin calls Guizot a "pamphleteer."

L. 132. Pierre Jean Beranger (1780-1857), the very popular author of French *chansons*.

58

L. 133. Pushkin names Rossini and Ferdinando Paër (1771-1839) as the composers of these arias. For some reason Paër's name is reduced to a monosyllable as "Per," perhaps to fit the metre.

L. 134. Pushkin has here, "Et cetera, et cetera" (in Latin script), but I could not rhyme this line.

Ll. 137-138. I have been forced to omit one line here: "Natalya Pavlovna, arising," since that lady's name and patronymic take up a total of six of the line's eight syllables, making a suitable rhyme almost impossible. To compensate I have added a line of my own improvization below (line 140).

L. 143. Actually the count moves not his chair but his place setting closer to the lady, but the term is awkward in English.

L. 145. I have changed Pushkin's "Holy Rus" to "Mother Rus," which is more familiar and funnier in English.

L. 150. François Joseph Talma (1763-1826), celebrated tragedian of the Comèdie Française, who in fact played for the last time in 1825 and left the stage to die the following year.

L. 151. Mlle. Mars (1779-1847), an actress of the Comèdie Française celebrated for her *ingénue* roles; she continued to play these as she grew older. At the time of the writing of "Count Nulin" she was thirty-six.

L. 152. Charles Potier (1775-1838), celebrated comic actor, who played in a number of vaudeville and comic theaters. I have followed Pushkin in rhyming "pitié" and Potier.

L. 156. Charles Victor Prévot, Vicomte d'Arlincourt (1789-1856), poet, novelist and dramatist. His long poem, *La Caroléide*, celebrated the Bourbon restoration. Alphonse de Lamartine (1790-1869), romantic poet, noted for the elevated philosophic and meditative tone of his lyrics. D'Arlincourt was hardly a very important writer, and it is possible that Pushkin names him because his trisyllabic name makes a good rhythmic counterpart to Lamartine's (which has the rhyme in the Russian original). Lamartine was more significant, and well known in Russia at the time, though Pushkin considered his rather pallid brand of Romanticism harmful. Kuechelbecker, Bestuzhev and, possibly, Baratynsky were influenced by him in their early attempts to introduce romantic poetry into Russia.

L. 166. *The Moscow Telegraph*, a miscellany, had just been launched in 1825, a few months before Pushkin wrote "Count Nulin." It featured a section on women's fashions, with a few illustrations in color.

L. 171. This line and the preceding four correspond to four lines only in the original, i.e., I have added a line here. I have managed to preserve two of the three enjambments in this passage.

L. 175. Literally, "Is amazed at how ingratiating (*mila*) she is."

L. 182. One might suppose that a certain time interval separates this line from the one two lines above.

L. 183. The nightwatchman beats with an iron clapper on a wooden board, as was the custom on Russian estates.

Ll. 202-3. Literally, "Now she expounds in serious fashion the count and his affairs."

L. 205. The verb here (*razvedat'*) implies that Parasha has been spying on the count. Unfortunately English lacks a verb with the meaning "spy and find out."

Ll. 210-211. I have largely invented these two lines; the original states that the count is undressed by his French valet.

L. 213. The name Picard is not rhymed here in the original, the word for "cigar" being *sigaru* (accusative case). However, the enjambment at the end of this line is found in the original.

Ll. 215-217. Pushkin also lists a silver cup; the "lamp" is actually a bronze candlestick; a carafe is mentioned intead of "wine," and the "clock" is an alarm-clock. The name Scott is rhymed in the original, but at the beginning of the following section.

Ll. 225-226. The enjambment here is my addition.

L. 235. Here Pushkin mentions his heroine's "pleasant voice, one truly womanly"; the epithet "womanly" I have transferred to her "look" two lines above.

L. 238. It is well known that Pushkin was a foot fetishist, but this subtlety of female adoration was doubtless more common then that it is today.

L. 240. An enjambment at the end of this line has been omitted.

L. 248. Pushkin mentions only a single chair that is knocked down, but perhaps the hyperbole does no harm.

L. 249. This and a succeeding allusion to Tarquin in line 279 suggest the parodic parallel with Roman history and Shakespeare's poem (see Introduction). The first version of Pushkin's poem was even entitled, "A Modern Tarquin."

L. 254. "As its just prey" is my own addition.

L. 256. "Half screwing up its eyes" is perhaps too literal a translation of the Russian *poluzazhmuryas'*, which implies that the eyes are partly closed to focus them better.

L. 257. Literally, "It twists itself into a ball and wags its tail."

Ll. 260-261. It is not clear at this point whether Nulin is still in his bedchamber or already in the corridor, but I could not resist the temptation to rhyme "gloom" and "room." The first line, with its suggestion of a tormented spirit wandering through Hell, is typical for Pushkin.

L. 266. The "catch" is made of brass, but the meter requires a two-syllable epithet, and I hesitated to use "brazen," with its strong secondary meaning. In this line and the next one I have utilized the English tendency for related words to rhyme (catch/latch), though there is no justification for the repetition in the original.

L. 276. Pushkin actually addresses the "ladies of Petersburg" here, but the phrase is awkward rhythmically, and the name Petersburg (or variants, such as "capital") supplied no usable rhyme.

L. 280. Pushkin describes the heroine's eyes as "large," but English lacks a bisyllabic adjective with that meaning, and I have had to omit the detail; I considered this preferable to the addition of an unjustified *cheville* (e.g., "large *blue* eyes").

L. 282. Literally, "He bestrews her with fancy feelings'" The word for ' "fancy" here is *vypisnye*, literally, "imported," "ordered from a distance."

L. 307. Count "Nocount"—see note on title.

L. 311. "Fine-toothed" is a *cheville*, but I thought it less harmful than "silver," "golden" or others that might have been employed.

L. 324. Literally, "He's jesting very agreeably," a Gallicism in Russian (*shutit ochen' milo*= il plaisante très agréablement).

L. 326. Literally, "Suddenly a noise in the corridor; someone enters. Who can it be?"—an enormous semantic burden for a single line of only nine syllables (in Russian). The narrative is ironically stylized here to resemble stage directions.

L. 336. The vodka is a gift from "far away," not of local manufacture and hence an object of curiosity and pleasant expectation. The detail is fairly subtle and difficult to convey in English.

Ll. 345-346. I have introduced an enjambment here that is not in the original.

L. 349. This line has been left unrhymed in Russian, perhaps as a whim of the author's. I have rhymed it, since the rhyme came very naturally, but I should point out that lines 346-347 just before have only a consonance in my translation (men/down), not an actual rhyme. Also, lines 23, 40 and 87 of my translation are unrhymed.

THE LITTLE HOUSE IN KOLOMNA

Like "Count Nulin," "The Little House in Kolomna" was written in a single burst of intense creativity, in the week between October 1 and 9, 1830. Pushkin wrote the poem on his estate at Boldino, near Nizhni Novgorod (today renamed Gorky) in the Volga country east of Moscow. He was spending the autumn of 1830 on his estate, confined there by a plague quarantine, restless and tormented by his longing to return to the life of Moscow and to his future bride, the beautiful Natalya Goncharova. As earlier during his exile at his estate of Mikhailovskoe, the enforced confinement proved salutary for his creation, and the fall at Boldino brought the production of some of his greatest works, including the last two chapters of *Eugene Onegin*, the four so-called "Little Tragedies," the prose *Tales of Belkin*, and the verse fairy-tale about the priest and his workman Balda, as well as some important lyrics.

Among this bounteous harvest of works, "The Little House in Kolomna" has always seemed in danger of getting lost, and it has been relatively neglected by Pushkin's critics, perhaps because they find it difficult to say anything very serious about it. In this they may reflect a certain resentment at the elaborate spoof the poem's plot provides. The poem was generally dismissed as worthless in Pushkin's own day, and it is clear that some readers did not even get the point of the narrative: that the cook Mavrusha is Parasha's lover in disguise!

And yet the poem is one of Pushkin's most significant, especially since its very conception is metapoetic, a poem about the making of poetry and poetic esthetics. For this reason the Russian Formalist critics valued it very highly; it illustrated better than anything else in Russian classic literature what the Formalist Victor Shklovsky called "laying bare the device," i.e., unmasking the illusion of reality by deliberately calling the reader's attention to the literary process it-

63

self. This had been a favorite procedure of such novelists as Fielding and Sterne, as it was to become a favorite device of Russian novelists of the 1920's such as Kaverin and Olesha. Pushkin's "Little House in Kolomna" served the Formalists as the canonical archetype of the device in older Russian literature.

Pushkin's initial intention was that the poem should remain unpublished, and he included a number of stanzas of literary musings and polemical matter, including some jabs at contemporary journals such as the *Literary Gazette* and the *Moscow Telegraph.* These he pruned from the poem's final version when he changed his mind and resolved to publish the work after all; the omissions were apparently made in 1833 when he did publish the poem, more because of the time lag, it would seem, than because of the sharpness of the polemical thrusts which he deleted. An inspection of the omitted stanzas (they are available in English in a translation by A.F.B. Clark in the *Slavonic and East European Review*, Vol. 15, July 1936, pp. 282-294) suggests that their elimination was rather the result of a careful pruning of what in fact was rambling and discursive matter, and the final form of the poem, with all its surviving digressions, is a good deal tighter for the effort. Pushkin had begun the work as a poem without narrative content, one that would deal only, in light-hearted fashion, with poetic and critical concerns and polemical matters; the story itself was virtually an afterthought, intended no doubt to illustrate the anti-romantic attitude which underlay his running polemic with the critics Polevoy and Nadezhdin. Once the narrative part was undertaken, the rather loose, digressive and allusive character of the metapoetic opening had to be brought under control: this especially in view of Pushkin's decision to publish the whole. It remains a question which of the two parts is more significant: the opening with its vigorous images of the poet marshalling his rhythms and rhymes like soldiers, or the tale, deliberately trivial, almost bathetic and limited by its anecdotal, one-joke plot. It would seem that Pushkin was determined to show that poetry could be fashioned out of any materials, even the most banal ones. Yet one should not undervalue the narrative in order to praise the uniqueness of the opening: the narrative too is relatively unique, especially in the context of its period (though Byron's "Beppo," in which there is also a disguise, and Pushkin's own "Count Nulin" are of course its prototypes). In the completed work the narrative portion is obviously essential to round out the metapoetic part, which might have seemed pointless if it had not been provided with an illustration of the poet's new artistic method.

The importance of "The Little House in Kolomna" for Pushkin's development rests in part, as with "Count Nulin," in its cultivation of the small detail, sometimes comic, sometimes trivial but "realistic," serving to fill out the literary space and make it striking, vivid and picturesque. Just as Pushkin had denied the literary cult of sentimentalism in the earlier poem (the endless novel his heroine reads on the love of Héloise and Armand), so he rejects both classicism and romanticism here. Classicism is put down in the metaliterary prologue ("The fountain's water which he [Pegasus] unlocked, dried up. And gone to seed Parnassus, while Zeus's aging daughters, the Muses, no longer tempt our breed."). The romanticism of the poseur, of the grand but hollow attitude that turns out on closer examination to be spiritually empty, is decisively rejected in the digressive episode involving Countess X and her cold pride, contrasted to the heroine Parasha's tender modesty and meekness. The story of Countess X (in life Countess Stroynovsky) must have fascinated Pushkin: a great beauty who came from a needy family of gentle birth, she had sacrificed herself to marry a rich old count of seventy, by which act she had recouped the family's fortunes and assured herself of a position in Petersburg society. Yet in the end Pushkin rejects her story in favor of Parasha's more humble and vulgar one. Indeed, the story makes a kind of poetry of the prosaic, and it is perhaps not accidental that it appeared at a time when Pushkin was beginning to turn away from poetry to prose, and at a time when he was polemicizing with Polevoy and Nadezhdin, who were seeking to import a high Romanticism from Western Europe into Russia.

It is true that nothing much comes from Parasha's story,

and the ending is unexpectedly trivial when compared with the brilliant opening or the fine stanzas that depict Parasha and her mother in their daily life in their tiny hovel. Pushkin rescues his story from banality by manifesting the same feigned ironic indifference with which he had ended "Count Nulin," but in fact the failure of his literary polemic to bring him to any positive esthetic outcome other than a rather banal, ironic and comic one might suggest that "The Little House in Kolomna" lies at the end of a blind alley for Pushkin: indeed the work has no sequel in his poetry, or even in his prose, if we discount the comic tale, "Mistress into Maid," in the *Tales of Belkin,* written a month before. But this is a reflection on the kind of mood and circumstance in the poet's work that produced the poem, and not on the poem itself. The statement of rejection of both classicism and romanticism were significant for a poet who had produced his "Poltava" only two years before), a poem that aspired to become the patriotic epic of the Russian people, but misses its mark because of a derivative and melodramatic false romanticism. Pushkin was to find his way out of this "blind alley" only several years later with his late, great "Bronze Horseman," his poetic masterpiece, and "The Little House in Kolomna," for all its mixture of styles and diverse elements, is an important stopping place along the artistic road that leads to that masterpiece.

Soviet critics have tended to define that final goal of Pushkin's poetic development as "realistic," and there is much evidence for realism in the choice of small details in both "Count Nulin" and "Kolomna," as well as in *Eugene Onegin.* But the solution is forced, and largely ignores the presence of persistent elements in his work that are irreconcilably opposed to a realistic tone. These include the frequent authorial digressions ("romantic irony") that serve to undercut the realistic assumption of an objective narrative and even the assumption of a smooth literary continuity and the unity of narrative and esthetic devices. For Pushkin well understood that poems are artifacts that reflect the craft and genius with which they are made, just as much as they are keys to the ultimate understanding of the cosmos. If we are to judge his final development by "The Bronze Horseman" rather than *O-negin* (and "The Bronze Horseman" was written some three years after *Onegin* was completed), then symbolism rather than realism might well be the name of the poetic style we would wish to settle for. But the terms are all arbitrary ones. Pushkin's creative development is unique, and this is part of its distinction: in "The Little House in Kolomna" he has made a rare, perhaps unique combination of "poetic" and "anti-poetic," of ironic, comic and prosaic elements that is one of the final achievements of his art.

Certain allusions in the poem, especially the poet's reference to his feeling of depression and rage at seeing a new three-storied house standing in place of Parasha's humble dwelling, are clearly personal, but have never been satisfactorily elucidated. Pushkin, who had lived in the Kolomna quarter of St. Petersburg in the years 1817-1820, had indeed visited the capital as recently as early August of 1830 (the poem was written in October of the same year), though this interval does not quite accord with the words "three days ago" which open Stanza X. Was his depression occasioned by the reflection that life was passing him by, that he had no permanent position, fortune, or even established literary reputation? Was his own fate to be as precarious as that of his heroine? He was engaged to marry the beautiful Natalya Goncharova, but the thought of impending wedded life brought him more disquiet than pleasurable anticipation. At Boldino, where he was cut off from his bride by the plague quarantine, he felt frustrated indeed. It would be tempting to try, as Gershenzon and Yermakov have done, to connect "The Little House in Kolomna" with Pushkin's separation from Natalya and his anxiety over the prospect of impending marriage, but such attempts to read the poem either personally or symbolically have invariably failed. Just possibly his seemingly exaggerated depression and rage were directed to uncertainty concerning his own role as poet and creator: would his work vanish as suddenly as that little house he hoped to immortalize? As a poet, was it his task to observe and record the world about him, or create a different world, in its own way immortal? Obviously a deep existential anxiety, imperfectly concealed behind Pushkin's customary mask of careless irony, pervades Stanzas X and XI, an anxiety or anxieties he was to confront more successfully later in "The Bronze Horseman."

For "The Little House in Kolomna" Pushkin used the poetic form of the octave (*ottava rima*), a complex verse form with triple rhymes that Byron had employed in both "Beppo" and *Don Juan*. Two narrative poems by Barry Cornwall, "Diego de Montilla" and "Gyges," both published in 1819, are also composed in octaves and, like Pushkin's "Kolomna," they both open with whimsical reflections on the poet's choice of meter; it seems beyond question that Pushkin knew one of these works or both of them. Intricate poetic forms were a challenge to Pushkin's fluent art of versification, and in *Onegin* he had already achieved the incredible feat of writing some 375 stanzas in an elaborate, sonnet-like form. The octave is composed in iambic pentameter (a longer line than Pushkin's favorite tetrameter, a form that he here specifically rejects), with the rhyme scheme abababcc. The triple rhymes a and b alternate as masculine and feminine in each stanza, in such a way that, save for the couplets, no two masculine or feminine rhymes ever fall in adjoining lines. All this formal complexity I have managed to retain, save that in the couplet rhyme I have arbitrarily opted for the best rhyme I could devise, masculine or feminine, rather than alternating these in successive stanzas as Pushkin does. I have taken this liberty for the sake of expressiveness, since the final couplet, as in *Onegin*, is important for the pithy and frequently witty filip it gives to the whole stanza, and these couplets and the quality of their rhymes probably help more to reproduce the characteristic Pushkinian tone than any other single detail. Like Pushkin, I have made very extensive use of enjambment in my translation, though not necessarily always in the same places. Pushkin's rhymes (unlike Byron's) are nearly always perfect ones, while I have been compelled to use some imperfect rhymes to fill in the triple sets. It must be pointed out that Stanza XXXVI has only seven lines in the original: in this stanza the masculine b rhyme occurs twice only. This metrical "oversight" on Pushkin's part is no doubt

deliberate, and resembles the series of dots which he publish-
ed to represent uncompleted stanzas of his *Onegin*. Perhaps
these omissions, like the single unrhymed line of "Count Nu-
lin," were made by him in order to demonstrate that the po-
et too is human, and to avoid the charge that he had created
a formal *tour de force*!

Connoisseurs of modern opera will no doubt recognize
the present poem as the source of the libretto of Stravinsky's
Mavra.

THE LITTLE HOUSE IN KOLOMNA

I

By now I'm all fed up with four-foot verse;
Each scribbler writes it. It's a mere diversion
For children—let them keep it. I could do worse
Than in the octave's measure make excursion.
5   It's true, in triple rhyme I'm little versed—
But let me try it. To fame I've no aversion!
For rhymes have ever echoed in my song!
Two come themselves: the third they'll bring along.

II

And so with types of rhyme I can't be choosy:
10   To verbal rhyme I'll grant the widest play.
You know, our poets past have oft refused it,
As though ashamed of it. Why so, I say?
True, S. of pious memory never used it,
And I eschew it too, whene'er I may.
15   Why should we so? Of rhymes we've scarce sufficient;
Without the verbs our rhyme will be deficient.

III

My armies with due rigor I'll impress;
The wounded I'll make serve without compunction,
For none of them is useless, I confess;
20   I'll even take the adverbs and conjunctions.
They're none too base to march under duress.
I need more rhymes; they all have their own functions.
For every word can serve in some *bon mot*;
We'll take them all, for we won't stand on show.

IV

25   Both masculines and feminines are needed!
Let's try it, trusting luck. So keep in step!
Dress up your ranks, yourselves keep time unheeded—
By threes the stanza's verses intercept.
Don't be afraid—you'll not be badly treated;
30   Look lively, and take care you don't misstep!
We'll quickly get the hang of it, God willing,
And soon there'll be some profit from our drilling.

V

How fine to march them dressed in war's array,
Parade them up and down in close formation.
35   And most important—not to let them stray
Lest they go off to their annihilation.
Here every word receives a hero's pay,
And every syllable a proud citation.
With whom shall poets then claim equal state?
40   With Caesar, or with Tamerlane the Great!

VI

Let's pause a while and make an intermission.
Shall we pull out, or rather up the stake?
I much prefer, since I'm a fair metrician,
After the second foot to place the break.
45   Else verse will seem a road in rough condition
(Although my sofa can't be said to shake):
Such lines are like a wagon rudely humping
As o'er the frozen plowland it goes bumping.

VII

And what's the harm? One can't forever stroll

50   Along the Nevsky, or rush to parties, avid
       To dance the night away, or riding bolt
       Across the Kirghiz steppe. So then I'll travel
       At gentle gait, but in a constant roll
       Like that eccentric, who, as gossips have it,
55   From Moscow to the Neva made his course,
       Not stopping on the way to feed his horse.

VIII

       The horse that made that journey was a trotter;
       But Pegasus could ne'er have caught him. That steed
       Is old and has no teeth. The fountain's water
60   Which he unlocked, dried up. And gone to seed
       Parnassus, while Zeus's aging daughters,
       The Muses, no longer tempt our breed.
       So we've forsworn Parnassus' lofty air,
       To pitch our tent right on the public square.

IX

65   Be quiet, Muse, and find yourself a seat;
       Tuck in your arms and legs. Don't fiddle!
       Time to begin. Eight years are now complete
       Since this took place. A poor but honest widow
       Dwelt with her daughter on a narrow street
70   Close by Pokróv; a sentry box stood vigil
       There. The house I see as 'twas before:
       A parlor, porch, three windows and a door.

X

       Three days ago I looked to rediscover
       That house, near which I strolled at evenfall.
75   It stood no longer. In its place another
       Rose loftier, a good three stories tall.

And by the window sat no more the mother
Nor the young girl, as them I oft recall
At evening time. I felt a slight misgiving—
80 Where were they now? Could they in fact be living?

XI

Reflection gave me pause; I looked askance
At what I saw. If that three-storied dwelling
Had flamed and burnt to ashes by some chance,
Then, all my discontented mood dispelling,
85 The flames had brought me joy. Conceits entrance
The heart at moments thus. Much that is repellant
Comes to the mind (which one should scarce attend)
Whene'er we roam, alone or with a friend.

XII

For they are blest who circumscribe speech tightly
90 And keep a leash on everything they think,
Who in their heart do ever silence rightly
The serpent's hiss and his eternal sting.
But him who chatters, rumor impolitely
Proclaims a scarecrow.... Lethe's draft I'll drink;
95 My doctor recommends it for depression:
Let's drop this talk—forgive my indiscretion.

XIII

The mother (a hundred times I've seen her guise
In poses such as Rembrandt liked to render)
Wore spectacles and bonnet. But the prize
100 Goes rather for the daughter's radiant splendor:
Jet black as night her tresses and her eyes;
Her skin was white, her look so soft and tender.
She had good taste, and loved to read some story,

73

So long as it concerned things amatory.

XIV

105   She played guitar and sang through many a ditty:
       She knew by heart, "There coos the woodland dove,"
       "When I go to the brook," and tunes as pretty;
       All those which tedious winters by the stove,
       Or autumns drear, by samovar long sitting,
110   Or in the spring, while strolling through some grove,
       To sing so sombrely our maids were born;
       Our Russian muse, you see, prefers to mourn.

XV

       I mean no metaphor: we are all doomed
       From drayman to top laureate, as a nation,
115   To sing a dirge. Our favorite mood is gloom—
       And so our Russian song. Notorious allegation!
       'Tis true: we start with hail! but of the tomb
       We sing before we're through. With desolation
       Our poems, like our songs, are all replete.
120   And yet their melancholy mood is sweet.

XVI

       Our beauty, it would seem, was named Parásha,
       And of the household had the total care:
       She sewed and knit, she did the family washing,
       And had the month's accounts all to prepare.
125   She supervised the boiling of the *kasha*
       (Their old cook Fyokla also had a share
       In this grave task, and did it very well,
       Though she had long since lost her sense of smell.)

74

XVII

130

The mother oft would sit by window sill,
By daytime light a woolen stocking knitting,
And in the eve at patience show her skill
Or tell one's fortune, at the table sitting.
The daughter, though, was ne'er a moment still,
Through house and yard she was forever flitting,

135

To everyone who passed her gaze receptive:
She noticed everything (O sex perceptive!).

XVIII

In winter early they the windows covered,
But kept in summer shutters open wide
Until late evening. Pale Diana hovered

140

Above the hut, and watched the girl inside.
(Without this sentence not a single lover
Can be depicted; thus it is prescribed!)
So evenings passed: while mother snored in sleep,
The daughter with the moon would vigil keep.

XIX

145

She heard the yowls of tomcats as they stalked
Across the roofs, their ladies serenading,
The watchman's far-off cry, the chime of clock,
But nothing more. Kolómna's night was laden
With peace and quiet. Now and then there walked

150

Two shadows, strolling arm in arm. The maiden
Lay silent now: her heartbeat could be heard
As under the stiff linen sheet it stirred.

XX

On Sundays they would leave their habitation

And toward the church, Pokróv, their journey make,
155 To stand in front of all the congregation
Left of the choir. No longer do I take
My walks there now, yet in imagination
(Is it in sleep, or am I still awake?)
I see Kolómna and Pokróv, and pass
160 My Sunday at a good old Russian mass.

XXI

There Countess X. to worship always came
(Her name has quite escaped my recollection),
Young, wealthy and enjoying beauty's fame,
Her entry pompous (such was her predilection).
165 Her prayers were haughty ones (she'd little shame!).
Ah! Sinner, I would gaze in her direction
And stare at her. Parasha stood quite near,
And looked, poor girl, beside her all too drear.

XXII

At times the lady, in disdainful splendor,
170 Would send a glance Parasha's way. But she
Continued quiet thanks to God to render
And did not turn the other's look to see.
She was th'epitome of meekness tender;
The lady, though, seemed wrapped in self-conceit,
175 In how she looked, in fashion's cult austere,
And in her beauty, haughty and severe.

XXIII

She seemed to be the perfect, cold ideal
Of vanity. Such was the indication;
But closer study of her gaze revealed
180 Another tale—of grief and resignation,

Of long misfortune... These signs she ill concealed,
And they it was which worked my fascination.
The countess, though, could scarcely realize
My true concern, and took me for love's prize.

XXIV

185 She suffered, though by fate she was created
A beauty; although her life's tale told
Of pleasured ease; to her was Fortune subjugated,
And Fashion its esteem did not withold
From her—and all the same she was ill-fated.
190 More blest than Countess X a hundred-fold
Parasha, as my reader will believe:
She was warm-hearted, if a bit naive.

XXV

Her braid a serpent on the comb of horn,
And serpentine her flaxen curls were sliding,
195 A dainty scarf o'er shoulders lightly thrown,
And round her neck her waxen beads were gliding—
A simple garb—but then before her home
Mustachioed guardsmen were forever riding:
She well knew how their notice to inspire
200 Without the aid of splendid, rich attire.

XXVI

But which of them had won her heart's affection,
Or whether to each one of them, instead,
She was indifferent? We'll see directly.
But up to now a peaceful life she'd led:
205 For balls she had no special predilection,
Nor even for the court (where, it was said,
A flunkey's wife was her quite close relation

And could have sent an invitation.)

XXVII

But soon their little household was bereaved:
210   Their cook came from the bath one evening ailing,
Took to her bed with chill. No time to grieve:
But vinegar, tea, spirit—all proved unavailing;
Even a poultice failed. On Christmas Eve
They said farewell to her. And then, unfailing,
215   The coffin came next morn, on Christmas Day,
To carry Fyokla's poor old corpse away.

XXVIII

Her absence from the household was regretted
By all—especially Puss. The widow feared
That they would hardly manage, unabetted—
220   Some two days, three, perhaps. No more, 'twas clear,
Could they to Heaven's mercy be indebted.
She called her daughter to her. "Parasha!" "Here!"
"We need a kitchen maid. But find one—where?
Let's ask our neighbor. Cheap ones are now so rare."

XXIX

225   "I'll ask her, Mama."   And so she left the house,
Bundling up warm. (The cold had not abated,
The snow crunched under foot; above no clouds;
The frosty air, star-studded, scintillated.)
The widow waited long; at last she drowsed
230   In her soft chair; the girl returned, belated,
And coming up to her said, "Mama, look,
I've brought you home a marvellous new cook."

XXX

There followed her afar, shuffling and scraping,
In simple short-cut pinafore begowned,
235 A maiden—tall, with figure not unshapely;
She crossed the room and gave a bow profound,
Then squeezed against the wall and
smoothed her apron.
"What will you take?" the widow, turning round,
Inquired of her. "Whate'er you deem as just,"
240 Came answer in a voice mild but robust.

XXXI

Her answer made a very good effect.
"And what's your name?" "It's Mavra."
"So, Mavrúsha,
Come live with us; you're young—be circumspect.
Chase off the men. My poor deceased Feklúsha
245 Was a real paragon in that respect.
Not once her virtue suffered diminution.
Serve us both well with diligence and zeal;
Be faithful and—but mind me well—don't steal."

XXXII

A day passed, two days, three. The girl proved able
250 To do but little: the food she cooked too soft
Or burnt; the china banged against the table
And broke; the meals she'd always oversalt.
To thread a needle she was quite unable;
She sulked and gave glum looks when
they found fault.
255 Of everything she made a proper mess;
To help Parasha strove without success.

79

XXXIII

On Sunday morn both ladies soon awaked
And went to church, to leave the maid behind
At home; the latter's teeth, you see, had ached
260 The whole night through. From suf-
                                    fering almost blind,
She hardly dragged about. Yet now a cake
She's getting ready, and cinnamon must grind.
They left her there. But as in church they prayed,
The widow suddenly became afraid.

XXXIV

265 She thought: "But why should such an inclination
For sweets appear so sudden in our maid?
Indeed she looks a real abomination.
Perhaps she stayed at home today, the jade,
To rob us and clear out? 'Twere ruination!
270 What will we do at New Year's? I'm so afraid!"
From fear the mother felt herself half dead.
At last, enduring it no more, she said:

XXXV

"Wait here, Parasha—something's worrying me!
I must run home and look." The daughter
                                    comprehended
275 No word of this. Her mother verily
Flew out as she the church front stairs descended.
Her heart beat as for some calamity.
She reached the hovel they'd left unattended:
The kitchen's empty. To her own room she sped,
280 And there she came upon—O horror, dread!

XXXVI

Before the mirror, in sedate position,
The cook was shaving. The widow gave a shriek
And sank down to the floor. The apparition
Leaped up and o'er her, still with soapy cheek
285   (Offending thus her widowèd condition),
Ran to the porch and down the stairs apace,
As thus she made escape, hiding her face.

XXXVII

The daughter soon arrived home from the service.
"What's wrong, Mama?" "Ah, you haven't heard!
290   Mavrushka..." "What about her then?" "Our servant...
I still can't quite believe it all occurred...
Her face all soapy...What a queer disturbance!"
"Excuse me, I can't grasp a single word.
But where's Mavrusha?" "Gone, and how depraved!
295   She—just like my lamented spouse—she shaved!"

XXXVIII

But if Parasha's face displayed alarm
I really can't say. No investigation
Could find the maid—the trail was hardly warm.
She'd gone, not claiming her remuneration,
300   But not inflicting any serious harm.
Who followed after her in her vocation
And served the ladies next? It's not my worry:
To end this tale I'm rather in a hurry.

XXXIX

"What! Can that be all? You're joking!"
                                 "Not really!"

305   "So this is where your octaves finally led!
           But why, then, did you beat your drum so freely,
           Recruit your men and step right out ahead?
           You picked a fitting line of march, now really!
           Couldn't you find another theme, instead?
310   And now, I'll bet, you won't supply a moral!"
           "No...or rather, yes, for let's not quarrel...

XL

           "Here is your lesson: I hardly see much sense
           In trying to hire a servant without paying.
           And if one's born a man, 'tis negligence
315   To dress up like a girl, without well weighing
           That fundamental law of nature, whence
           A man who hides in skirts needs time for shaving.
           For beards ill suit a woman's reputation.
           No more will you extract from my narration."

Title. *Domik v Kolomne*, "The Little House in Kolomna." "Cottage" might be more idiomatic in English, but a cottage implies a situation in the country. Besides *domik* ("small house"), Pushkin several times uses the word *lachuzhka*, "hovel," which would be more precise, save that the word lacks the fullness and ring essential in titles.

Kolomna is the quarter of St. Petersburg along the right bank of the Fontanka River, a branch of the Neva. Pushkin had lived there with his parents in the period 1817-1820, between his student days and his southern exile.

Ll. 1-8. Iambic tetrameter had been the staple verse of Pushkin's narrative poetry up to this point, though, as we have seen, he had used iambic pentameter in the *Gavriiliada* as well as in his dramatic poetry. The octave (Italian *ottava rima*) called for iambic pentameter with a rhyming sequence abababcc, including two sets of triple rhymes. Pushkin undoubtedly took the form from Byron and Barry Cornwall (see Introduction); like Byron, Pushkin employs the form for a humorous, epigrammatic narrative with many personal digressions.

Ll. 3-6. Pushkin here confesses that for a long time he has wanted to use the octave, and to master the triple rhyme. It should be pointed out, however, that he had made occasional use of triple rhymes in both the *Gavriiliada* and "Count Nulin."

L. 13. The original contains no name, but an omission of three syllables with the stress on the second syllable. Commentators have long since indentified the name in question as that of the poetaster Shikhmatov: Prince S.A. Shirinski-Shikhmatov (1785-1837) was a high official of the period who wrote religious poetry (hence the ironic epithet of *bogomol'ny*, "pious," which Pushkin applies to him). He opposed the use of verbal rhymes. In a letter written to Kuchelbecker in December, 1825, Pushkin called Shikhmatov a "boring windbag (*skuchnii pustomelya*)." As a partisan of the archaist camp led by Admiral Shishkov, Shikhmatov belonged to the party of Pushkin's literary opponents, but it must be confessed that in his distaste for rhyming verb endings, he was taking a more progressive position than Pushkin. Still, Pushkin needed as many triple rhymes as possible for his octaves, and the poetic polemic implied here is scarcely to be taken very seriously.

Ll. 17-19. Literally, "I won't be too choosy in turning them [the rhymes] down, like draftees who are invalided, or like horses, for poor form."

L. 23. Literally, "I'll even take the whole *Dictionary*; whatever is made up of syllables can serve as a soldier."

L. 40. Pushkin mentions Tamerlane and Napoleon here, but not Caesar.

Ll. 44-48. Pushkin uses the term "caesura" here to denote his customary pause after the fourth syllable of the line (in both his iambic tetrameter and pentameter), but I have been unable to incorporate this not very poetic term in a suitable line; moreover, the temptation to rhyme "break" was overwhelming. It must be noted that line 44 does not have a "break" after the fourth syllable of the original, but after the fifth; I have had to sacrifice this deliberately "rough" effect here, but have retained it in lines 46-48 (Pushkin also has it in lines 47-48).

L. 57. Pushkin had already used the term "trotter" (*rysak*) in line 55, so that I have felt it advisable to make the term more explicit here than he does. Pegasus is described as an "ambler" (*inokhodets*); the whole conceit plays on the contrast between an empty classicism (which Pushkin had already discarded), and a "new" poetry of everyday but picturesque details.

L. 61. A reference to Phoebus Apollo, now living in retirement, has been omitted here by me.

L. 68. "Honest" is a *cheville* which completes the usual cliche.

Ll. 69-70. Pushkin calls the house a "hovel" (*lachuzhka*) here; the detail of the "narrow street" is my own addition. Pokrov is the name of a church in the quarter, on the corner of Sadovaya Street and Angliiski Prospekt.

L. 74. Pushkin mentions that he was strolling there "with an acquaintance."

L. 86. Literally, "much that is nonsense."

L. 101. Pushkin rather mentions here "eyes and brows."

Ll. 103-104. Literally, "She had educated taste," i.e., she was able to read the not very good but pretentious Russian fiction of the day; I have perhaps made the irony overly explicit in calling attention to her "good" (actually "poor" or "misguided") taste. Line 104 tells us that she was fond of the works of Fedor Emin (ca. 1735-1770), a Russian writer of endless epistolary novels.

Ll. 106-107. These are the first lines of two popular sentimental romances, stylized in the folk-song manner, the first by I.I. Dmitriev (1760-1837), the second by Y.A. Neledinsky-Meletsky (1752-1829). Actually the woodland dove "groans," a folk turn of phrase following from the fact that the bird represents melancholy and grief.

L. 107. Literally, "and that which of old."

L. 113. Literally, "Figuratively or literally."

L. 121. Pushkin also rhymes the name Parasha here (with *nasha*, "our" and *kasha*, "porridge"); I have retained the rhyme with *Kasha*.

L. 128. Actually she had lost her sense of hearing as well.

Ll. 141-142. Literally, "Without this phrase not a single novel can make do; so it is prescribed."

L. 156. "Left of the choir"; actually, the choir may be arranged on both sides of the altar in a Russian Orthodox Church, so that the sense is probably, "by the left section of the choir."

Ll. 156-157. Pushkin says literally, "No longer do I live there now" (see note on the title above).

L. 161. Countess X, actually Countess Stroynovsky (see Introduction).

L. 165. Literally, "She prayed haughtily (she was indeed haughty!)"

L. 192. The phrase, "if a bit naive" is my own addition.

L. 195. Literally, "Her scarf worn crosswise or tied in a knot."

L. 205. Literally, "Without thinking either of balls or of Paris."

Ll. 206-208. The relative in question is actually a first cousin named Vera Ivanovna, the wife of a court *goffyuryer*, a supervisor over flunkeys who had relatively high seniority in the service heirarchy entitling him to certain perquisites and privileges. Pushkin rhymes the name Vera and the genitive case form, *goffyuryera,* for the final couplet, but I could not follow him here, and was forced to improvise line 208 anew; this line is entirely my own invention.

Ll. 214-216. Saying farewell *(prostit'sya)* to the dying is a part of prescribed Russian ritual. The cook actually died on the night of Christmas Eve and the coffin came "that very day," i.e., on Christmas Day. Fyokla was buried in the paupers' cemetery at Okhta, on the edge of Petersburg.

L. 232. "Marvellous" and "new" are my own *chevilles*.

L. 233. Literally, "There followed her, coming forward timidly."

L. 235. Probably, Pushkin is referring to the face when he says that the girl is "not bad looking," rather than to the figure, as I have it.

L. 239. Literally, "Whatever you may please."

L. 242. Pushkin also rhymes the diminutive name Mavrusha with Feklusha (as I have it) and *narusha*, "violating."

Ll. 245-246. Literally, "Served me as cook ten years, not once violating the duty of honor."

L. 248. Literally, "Be zealous; don't cheat on the accounts."

L. 256. Literally, "[No matter how much] Parasha strove, she could not smooth things out."

L. 270. The Christmas and New Year season is a major holiday in Russia, requiring elaborate preparation, especially in the kitchen.

Ll. 272-273. Pushkin runs Stanza 34 and 35 together without a full stop, as I do.

L. 283. The word "apparition" is my own.

Ll. 285-286. This stanza has only seven lines in the original (see Introduction); the third instance of the b rhyme is therefore lacking.

L. 286. Literally, "Sprang to the entry (*seni*) and out onto the stairs."

L. 289. "Mamá" is probably too affected for Parasha, who has been saying "Máma" in my translation up to now; in fact she says *mamen'ka* in Russian at this point.

L. 292. "What a queer disturbance" is my own addition.

Ll. 314-318. Literally, "And if one's born a man, it's strange and foolish for him to put on skirts: some day he'll have to shave his beard, a thing which ill accords with women's nature..."